Stories of My Life:
The Search for True Love

by

Elisabeth M. Seidel

Edited by Jennifer P. Tanabe

Copyright © 2019 Elisabeth M. Seidel

All rights reserved.

ISBN 978-0-359-65235-8

"Love is patient, love is kind. It does not envy, it does not boast, it is not proud. It is not rude, it is not self-seeking, it is not easily angered, it keeps no records of wrong. Love does not delight in evil but rejoices with the truth. It always protects, always trusts, always hopes, always perseveres. Love never fails."

1 Corinthians 13:4-8

Merry Christmas 2003 Mom!

I Love You.

- Diesa

Table of Contents

Introduction 9
Autobiography 13
Childhood 23
    My Biggest Tribe 25
    The Orphanage in Lyon 29
    Family Stories 32
    Cousin Renée's Tales 34
    Her Life Was not a Peaceful River 37
    Parce que c'est ma mère 40
    A Teenager's Dream 42
Early Years in the Unification Movement 45
    Becoming a Member of the Unification Church 50
    My Experiences with Our True Parents in Paris 53
    The Shoes My Father Bought 60
    Letter to Missionaries 61
    Prayer at Town Hall of Paris 5th Arrondissement 64
    Prayer at Town Hall of Paris 7th Arrondissement 67
    Prayer on the Way to Charles de Gaulle Airport 69
    About Christiane Coste 71
    Journal Entries 1976 – 1978 in New York 73
        June 8, 1976: *America – Land that We Love* 75
        June 14, 1976: About the Kingdom of God 76

June 15, 1976: The Power of Positive Thoughts 77
June 27, 1976: The Most Important Thing is Love 78
June 29, 1976: A New Heart for Spiritual Children 80
July 3, 1976: Education of the Heart 81
July 12, 1976: God Loves Me 81
July 16, 1976: The Husband God Will Choose for Me 82
July 20, 1976: True Mother's Inner Peace and Prayers 83
July 24, 1976: Heavenly Heart 83
October 3, 1976: Washington Monument 84
November 27, 1976: To Be Like True Parents 85
December 1, 1976: Finding Spiritual Children 85
December 13, 1976: I Met God 86
December 24, 1976: True Parents Are Shining 87
December 26, 1976: Christmas with True Parents 88
December 28, 1976: Comfort Brothers and Sisters 88
December 31, 1976: God's Day, 1977 89
January 25, 1977: To Love Any Person 90
February 4, 1977: Rumors of a Blessing 90
February 9, 1977: We Feel Happy and Protected when True Parents Are Around 92
February 16, 1977: My Life of Sins Passed Away 92
February 18, 1977: The Matching 94
March 4, 1977: The Blessing 95
March 16, 1977: Warm Hearts 97
March 22, 1977: A Most Romantic Husband 97
March 31, 1977: Unity is the Key to Success 98

May 9, 1977: Love Can Cure Everything 99

May 12, 1977: So Grateful 100

May 24, 1977: Saving New York 100

May 30, 1977: My Handsome Husband 101

June 13, 1977: Nobody Came 103

June 16, 1977: Forgive, Love, Unite 103

June 23, 1977: Persecution and Love 104

September 5, 1977: The One Who Makes Our Dreams Come True 104

October 5, 1977: Dreams of True Parents 105

February 28, 1978: Concerning Christiane Coste 107

In Canada 109

Our Canadian Mission 111

Journal Entries 1980 – 1984 120

November 16, 1980: The Origin of Love and Peace 122

November 17, 1980: The Tragedy of the Fall of Man 122

December, 1981: As you Loved Me, Love one Another 123

December 26, 1981: Heavenly Father, Our Parent 126

December 31, 1981: The Light of Beautiful Canaan 127

April 20, 1982: Praying for Christianity 128

June 25, 1982: The Joys and Tears of Fundraising 129

June 29, 1982: Dr. Kryspin 131

July 14, 1982: "Moonie, No Thank you" 132

July 24, 1982: Meetings in our Home 132

July 30, 1982: I Need God and God Needs Me 133

August 2, 1982: How to Touch People with a True Heart . 135

August 31, 1982: Dream of the Kings of France 135

December 7, 1982: Comfort through the Crickets 136

February 28, 1983: In the Hands of God 136

March 7, 1983: Making God's Heart Joyful 137

March 10, 1983: Raising our Children 138

January 27, 1984: Dream of True Parents 139

Letter to Father Moon 141

Later Years in the Unification Movement 153

At the Pond 156

Visits to Ministers, Spring 1989 157

Journal Entries 1988 – 1990 159

Easter Sunday - April 3, 1988: Return to Belvedere 161

June 29, 1988: Father Signed Dietrich's Thesis 164

May 26, 1989: Coke, Favorite Drink of Hyun Jin nim 167

May 31, 1989: Another Cake by Marie France 168

September 1, 1989: $100 Bill 168

December 23, 1989: More to Eat 169

March 22, 1990: We All Have to Grow 170

Letter to Friends, December 7, 1989........................171

Letter to Friends, December 17, 1991 174

Prayer to Conclude 1997 176

Reconciliation and Mending of Relationships between France and Austria-Germany in My Own Family 177

The River of Life Goes On............................... 185

Family..187

 Interview with Dietrich's Mother, 2006 .... *188*

 My Dad *193*

 On Dying Alone *195*

 Orphans and Orphanages *196*

 I am Your Child, Please Always Check on Me *198*

 I am Always Grateful *198*

 On Gratitude *199*

 The Escapades of Oma and Gisela *200*

 The Great Love *204*

Persecution and Reconciliation **206**

 Visit to the Holy Land *207*

 Letter of Repentance *208*

 It Happened to Me *209*

 True Love Will Prevail *211*

 Claiming Back my Hometown *212*

 Don't Worry, Be Happy, Mamas *214*

Ecumenical Work **216**

 At the Shooters Restaurant *217*

 September 2013 Prayer on the Occasion of Dietrich's 70th Birthday, with our Syrian Friends in Vienna *218*

 Petition to Heaven *220*

 Chapelle Sainte Marguerite *221*

Restoration of Beloved France **223**

 Where Is France Going? *224*

 Holy Ground in Savoie *225*

 Letter to My Friend in Lyon *227*

Tribute to Bernadette Bellay Sattlberger 229
Eternal Father of France 231
Reflections on the Life of Reiner Vincenz 233

Living with God 235
I Knew God Must Exist 236
Meaning of Christmas 237
Christmas Visit 238
Healing Power 239
Isolation Is Hell 240
Evergreens by My House 242
The Woman Who Knew the Taste of God's Tears 243
The Geese – Why We Should Learn from Them 244
How We Start our Day Sets the Tone for the Whole Day .. 246

Help from Heaven 248
God's Blessings Come in Unexpected Ways 249
Angels' Help 250
Dreams and Angels in Our Life Again 251
Signs from Above 255

Dietrich, Eternal Loving Spouse 257
Concluding 1997 258
Our Treasures in Heaven 260
Dear Donor 262
It Is Very Natural 262
San Diego Beach Where Heaven and Earth Meet 265
Let's Go Somewhere 266
When I Need You, You Are Around 266

I Had a Dream 267

The Stadt Park in Vienna 268

When the Night Comes 270

Love Needs to be Expressed Over and Over and Beyond this World 271

Dear Dietrich 271

Recommended Readings 275

Introduction

When I was asked by Elisabeth Seidel (née Jamen) to help her publish this memoir, aptly entitled "Stories of My Life," I did not know what to expect. Although I knew much of her life, I also knew that I would learn many new things about her through these stories. That was certainly true!

One of Elisabeth's stories is called "Her Life was not a Peaceful River," and it tells the story of her mother's life. Her comparison of life to a river gave me inspiration for working on this project.

It is often said that life can be compared to a river. Each person's life takes a different course, but they all head towards the ocean, no matter what we do. There are obstacles on that course, some natural like waterfalls and eddies and rapids, and others are man-made like dams. But water always finds a way, and so the river always reaches the ocean.

In Elisabeth's stories I learned how she encountered obstacles. There were the turbulent rapids where everything moves so fast and one mistake can be disastrous, the deep pools where there is so much to learn, the painful moments when there is no rain and the river dries up, and the playful sections where the water ripples in the sunlight and it is never boring and always delightful. Then there were the waterfalls, the moments in life when everything is turned upside down without warning and the tears pour down from your eyes. A waterfall is a beautiful thing, when viewed from a safe distance! But when it comes upon you suddenly, when you least expect it, the effect is one of shock and even terror. But if you survive, as Elisabeth did, you can look back in amazement at its beauty and how it enhances the river of your life for the future.

Editing Elisabeth's writings was like moving the stones and rocks in the river and finding the treasures beneath. In some cases, those things were buried for a reason; some might even say, better to remain buried. But the true worth of a person's life is found in how they overcome the difficulties and continue their course to their destination.

What is that ocean, the destination that our rivers are flowing inexorably towards? Many people have no answer, but just drift along hoping for the best. Others are fearful and resist the inevitable changes in their lives. For Elisabeth, the dream of her childhood to find true love has always been the destination of her river. At first she traveled, seeking the purpose of her life in distant and romantic places. Then, through meeting members of the Unification Church, she encountered the love of God, and God's purpose of creation for humankind – true love.

From that time, armed with a selfless faith, Elisabeth has spent her life facing numerous challenges in her quest to bring God's true love to all humankind. God's love has been with her throughout, expressed most clearly through her beloved husband, Dietrich, with whom she spent forty years on this earth. Their love continues to unite them after his passing over into the eternal spiritual realm.

These stories of Elisabeth's life include reflections, journal entries, letters, reports, prayers and poems. Some of the reports and letters were originally written in French and translated into English for this book. The poems are especially beautiful because her artistic side comes out naturally. But there is beauty in all her writings. There are also deep insights into God's providence and how the love of God reaches each person here on earth and in the eternal realm.

The book begins with her autobiography, which provides a kind of road map for the reader to show where her life's travels took her. Then the main content is divided into five sections: "Childhood," which includes stories about her parents and grandparents and other relatives; "Early Years in the Unification Movement," which offers a window into the life of early Western followers of Revered Sun Myung Moon; "In Canada," which contains many details of her early married life and the birth of her children; "Later Years in the Unification Movement," in which we learn of Elisabeth's outreach efforts to various sectors of society, including her own family; and the final section, entitled "The River of Life Goes On," contains reflections on events later in her life. At the beginning of each section I have added a brief introduction which explains key events and concepts, particularly those referring to the Unification Movement.

As an editor, I was faced with the challenge of knowing when to keep the original writing and when to correct the grammar of a non-native English speaker – Elisabeth having been born and raised in France speaks excellent English with a French flair! The effort to keep her original "voice" must be balanced with the desire to present her writings in the best possible light to the English reader.

It has been an honor to read Elisabeth's life stories. I hope this publication provides great inspiration to many readers.

Jennifer P. Tanabe, Ph.D.

Red Hook, New York, May, 2019

Autobiography

I was born on October 18, 1945 in a small French town in the Alps. I grew up as a child in La Chambre, a village in Savoie in the French Alps, beautiful and close to nature.

When I go back to Chambery (where I was born), St. Jean de Maurienne (where I received my teenage education), or La Chambre, I feel that they are all my hometowns. I go back with an American spirit and with my father's love and my mother's love. I love France very much and cry over this country, how the revolution of 1789 and the resulting affairs of state now have separated this nation from God.

Chambery, where Elisabeth was born

My family, with many stories of the horrors of World War II and the crimes of the Germans, shaped my thinking as a young person. However, the most important thing, which I remember vividly, is that my father forbade me to go to church. Every day on my way to school I would pass the Catholic Church by crossing over to the other side of the street, thus avoiding being in front of the church and following my father's direction.

I became intrigued and anxious to know what it is that they teach there that I am not allowed to know. All my school friends were going there on Sundays and Thursdays when school was out. I heard conversations such as, "Satan will take you, if you do not go to church." My father said I could choose my religion when I was 18 years old.

My family went through a lot of turmoil and my parents divorced when I was 17. I would tell my school friends that I would travel around the world and find something marvelous – I would find the truth. They looked at me in amazement. So, I went to work and to study in Greece, England, France and Italy. I felt some spiritual guidance in the summer of 1970 when I worked as a tourist guide. I took people to vacation spots, and again this intuition came over me that I would find the truth. But I would have to work hard; my life would not be easy. So, during the last week at the vacation spot, I delighted in the ocean water under the sun at the island of Minorca in Spain, enjoying a beautiful vacation before starting my life mission.

I returned to Milano, where I shared an apartment with a former Catholic nun. Although we were both in our early twenties, she already had the experience of a religious life. I had many questions, such as "Does God exist?" "Is there life after death?" "Where can I find true love?" She said she knew a group who could answer all my questions but, because I did not have a religious upbringing, I would not be able to understand their teaching. I insisted that she please give me the address of this group, but for a long time she resisted. She said all her life she was told Jesus came to die for us, and now they said he should not have died. It was not necessary for Jesus to be crucified.

Finally, after pleading with her, she gave me the phone number of the Unified Family, or the Holy Spirit Association for the Unification of World Christianity (HSA-UWC). I called right away and was asked to come the following week for a conference. I asked if I could come immediately, but I was told to wait. Finally, the D-day came and I became very excited and very happy. I remember that I had just found the coat of my grandmother Marie, when I was visiting my parents in France, and I took the coat with me as it was again in fashion.

It was October 1970. I put on the coat and ran to the place. I interrupted my run to dance in the street. The atmosphere seemed so high, like many people were with me rejoicing. I entered the center and immediately walked towards the picture of a man and asked "Who is he?" I was told, you will know after you understand his teaching. On the bottom of the picture was written, "I will teach you how to pray." It was a black and white picture.

For a couple of months, I went there a few times every week to study the Divine Principle in the Italian language. At the conclusion of the teaching, I felt shaken and at the same time I really wanted to connect deeply. Unfortunately, the national leader of the Unification Movement in Italy at that time, Reverend Martin Porter, had to close down the Milano center. So again, I was faced with an obstacle – what should I do? I decided to ask my boss at the tourist agency to send me to Paris for Christmas with some Italian tourists. Although I did not want to go there, I figured out that I could contact this group and continue my study of the Divine Principle in Paris.

I arrived in Paris one evening at the HSA-UWC headquarters, situated on the Rue le Sueur (Road of Sweat) in the 16th district, and asked if I could resume my studies. They asked me to wait at the door for a while. I found out later that they thought I was a spy and were wondering if they should let me in. They did let me in, and for the following week I studied every night with Reverend Reiner Vincenz, who became my spiritual father. I suddenly felt many tears coming. I cried non-stop. I could not stop crying. Every night I cried. The teaching was intense and I felt the burden of God for the whole world. We were a bunch of youngsters to whom was given a new revelation to save the world. It was so overwhelming. I had to learn to compose myself again and go back to Italy to quit my job, give away my stuff, burn the letters which belonged to my past and make a fresh start in Paris.

God's Day,[1] January 1st 1971, is very special for me. Reiner asked me to be there for the midnight prayer on December 31st, 1970, the beginning of my spiritual birthday. I had to arrange with my colleague that she would take over my job to show Paris to the tourists, so that I could attend this prayer meeting and start the New Year with God. I had to run through Paris because the roads were blocked for the New Year festivities beginning at midnight. I ran all the way to the church center, arriving one minute before midnight with relief in my heart. I made it on time.

The members were making conditions to have a membership of 21 by God's Day, 1971. I was among the few who joined at that time. My life became a religious life, strict, rigid, with many days of fasting, a lot of prayers, hard work and little sleep. To top all of this, there were many spiritual attacks and physical attacks as well. We worked during the day and witnessed at night. On the weekend, we made many sacrificial conditions, like going to the small suburbs of Paris with no food or lodging, or praying while walking around Paris the whole night.

---

[1] God's Day, the first day of the new year, is a holy day in the Unification Movement.

We had signs in St. German des Pres, the Latin quarter (student quarter). We walked with signs on our backs saying "The Messiah is on earth." The communists in France in the 1970s were powerful and violent. One night in Lyon, as Mr. Henri Blanchard was giving a talk in a public place, they physically forced us to leave.

I found 12 spiritual children in about two years' time, and then I worked as a secretary at the French Headquarters for Reiner Vincenz and later for Henri Blanchard. I mainly helped members to be stable through spiritual guidance and counseling. European teams started and we received many threatening phone calls at our small HQ apartment. Communists wanted to bomb our place. Being filled with prayers, having faith, being innocent youths and a bit naïve, we would go to the kitchen in the basement, or to the hallway and wait. At one point, one center in Paris was bombed during the night and a sister lost part of her arm. It was a great shock for the membership. The European team was staying at that same place.

In 1976, I moved to America and participated in the Washington Monument and Yankee Stadium campaigns.[2] At the end of the year I had a dramatic car accident in New York while I was crossing the street. As the pedestrian light was changing from red to green, a car tried to beat the light and came full speed towards me, hit me in the back and I was thrown on the ground. In one split second, I was praying to God "My life is for you." The car rolled over my body and I sensed the car being lifted up at the places that could have hurt me, as if a band of angels were there to help me.

---

[2] Unification missionaries invited the public to attend Reverend Moon's speeches at Yankee Stadium in New York and Washington Monument in Washington DC.

The driver came out of his car and shouted at me. Then he left. There was a crowd around me, looking at me, seeing how much I was hurt. One man said he called an ambulance. A lady sat beside me waiting for the ambulance and she said, "I saw Jesus and he saved your life." Still semi-unconscious with some internal injuries and a broken arm, I never forgot what the lady said. After a few days at the hospital, I slowly recovered and renewed my faith. My love for God became stronger, including my love towards True Parents and all humankind.

A couple of months later, Father Moon announced a Matching and Blessing[3] to take place in February 1977. Colonel Bo Hi Pak said to me, looking at my arm, "after a big indemnity comes a big blessing." I truly experienced the love of God at the Matching and Blessing ceremony. When introduced to my husband, Dietrich, and looking deeply into his eyes, it was like a spiritual experience going through a tunnel all the way to heaven and sensing God and His profound love. God was looking at me through Dietrich.

For these two days of celebration, I truly experienced the kingdom of God on earth. I was smiling non-stop so that a few days later I even felt cramps from smiling too much. As the 74 Couple Blessing group at the New Yorker Hotel, we felt close to each other as true brothers and sisters. Tasting God's love through True Parents[4] at the Blessing ceremony is the

---

[3] Reverend Moon acted as a matchmaker, introducing potential marriage partners from single members of the Unification Movement who wished to receive the Holy Marriage Blessing. More details of this process are included in the Introduction to the section "Early Years in the Unification Movement."

[4] Reverend and Mrs. Moon are often referred to as "True Parents" by members of the Unification Movement.

peak of one's life. Our couple was from Austrian-German and French backgrounds, and we were well aware of the enmities between our nations. We were working for world peace and God's kingdom on this earth, thus on the way all things needed to be healed with lots of forgiveness, repentance and new beginnings.

From the first class of seminarians at the Unification Theological Seminary, Father Moon chose 12 students to study for a Ph.D. degree and my husband, representing Austria, was one of them. Thus, Dietrich and I started our family life in Toronto, Canada. We had many students from the University of Toronto who came to our apartment, and we taught them the Divine Principle and showed many videos about our Unification movement. I recall that professors also came and wanted to know more about Reverend Moon. We even had one TV interview.

Our children, Christopher and Diesa, were born in Toronto. I will always remember going with my babies to visit professors in their offices to tell them about our church. We had good relationships with the professors, and hosted several events for them in our apartment or the church center. In 1987 we moved to the Unification Theological Seminary (UTS) in Barrytown, New York, where Dietrich began teaching theology courses.

We continued witnessing and organized the Community Dinner Talks and took care of student families. Also, we responded to the need for taking care of ministers with Interfaith Prayer Breakfasts and marriage and family seminars, which initially started at UTS and then moved to our home. Father Moon gave us the blueprint of how to live in the kingdom of God and we could experience God's love and the love of True Parents.

How can we love people so that they too can experience the true love of God as we did? Despite rejection, mockery and attacks, we still love people. As I look back, beyond teaching the Divine Principle comes the love of God. Loving relationships come before teachings. True Love is a decision not just a feeling. In our tribal mission work now in Europe, we first make sure that everybody feels like part of the "family" like children do. Our reconciliation events between France and Austria-Germany bring many people together and we share our hearts at these events, giving out Ambassador for Peace awards while creating eternal loving relationships and taking away any traces of resentment.

I never ever thought that this path could be so difficult, that so much pain, so many tears and heartaches would be my destiny for following a religious life. I never thought it would be so difficult to follow those whom God had sent as the Messiah, the returning Lord, the true Man, the Savior for all religions and the True Parents of heaven, earth and humankind.

How fortunate I am to have recognized the True Parents. I thank my angels, my spirit guides and all the helpers who work with me, saving me from attacks and dangers, and always finding hope again and trust and faith. During over 40 years I never doubted and always had faith.

Thank you, True Parents.

The highest purpose of life is to be born through love, be raised in love, and to leave love behind

~ Sun Myung Moon

Childhood

In these essays we learn about Elisabeth's early years, the lives of her parents and their parents, and other members of her extended family. This turns out to be as many as 400 people!

The stories of her family are troubled, filled with difficulties and sadness, with painful disappointments and unfulfilled dreams. Still, Elisabeth's dream of finding true love was born in the mountains of Savoie, a dream that sustained her through her own years of challenges.

The French Alps where Elisabeth grew up

The Alps have their own majesty and strength. Perhaps they were a source of strength for those in Elisabeth's family, when they felt a lack of love from those who should have loved and cherished them.

We learn that Elisabeth was able to find the beauty and value in each person in her family, especially her mother for whom she wrote a wonderful poem. That poem is included here in both the original French and the English translation: "Parce que c'est ma mère (Because it's my mother)."

Elisabeth as a young child

My Biggest Tribe

My great-grandmother, Marie Virginie Milleret, and great-grandfather, Charles, had 12 children. Marie died when her last child was born. She was still very young.

For both my grandmother, Elisabeth, and my grandfather, Jules Bartholomé, it was a second marriage. Elisabeth's spouse died during the war and Jules had also lost his wife.

Elisabeth, with some of her extended family

All my relatives from Elisabeth and Jules come from a small village in the mountains called Montaimont in Savoie. I never came to know my grandmother Elisabeth, as she died when my mother was 13 years old. All the children of her 12 brothers and sisters know each other and are good friends.

When we had a family reunion one summer, we counted 400 people in our tribe of relatives. Now of course many have passed away.

My mother was raised by her father and the neighbor family next door. She became best friends with their daughter, Ginette. These two families stayed good friends all their lives, always coming to each other's homes. One son of Ginette, Bernard, and my brother Yves also became best friends.

It is indeed very special to love each other's family and care for each other in such a way, like being an extended family. I remember when I was a child going to their home any time I wanted to. I just had to cross the street.

Neighbors Lucienne and Dede Didier

Lucienne, one of the daughters in this family, was an extraordinary cook. I have in my mind one dessert she would make with fruit salad and lots of cherries inside. Those red cherries I remember vividly floating on top of the fruit salad. Maybe this is why cherries are my favorite fruit. When the season comes, I eat them every day.

School children in La Chambre. Elisabeth is seated front center, with darker jacket.

When I was going to elementary school, there was a cherry tree at another neighbor's house. The branches bent over our courtyard and each morning my mother would pick them and these were most delicious and fresh. How I love cherries! Maybe they carry the happy memories of my childhood in that village.

Elisabeth with her brother, Yves, as children

The Orphanage in Lyon

My other grandma, Marie (Thomas) Jamen, loved me very much. I loved her very much too. This is the story as she told it to me.

She became an orphan when her mother dropped her off at an orphanage in Lyon. She did not talk much about her earlier years there, but when she was a young child, maybe eight or nine, she was invited for the summer to a family in Saint Etienne de Cuines, Savoie, to help work in the fields. This family was very good to her.

When the summer ended, the family brought her to the train to go back to the orphanage. But at the train station my Grandma made a big scene, holding the couple and crying, refusing to enter the train to go back to the orphanage. So, from this day on, the couple decided to adopt my Grandma. She always said how good they were to her and all the other children too.

She married my grandfather Jean Baptiste when they were both very young. My Grandpa was 25, and he had no more relatives except his brother, 20 years older than him, who raised him, as he did not know who his father was.

They had two children, Yvonne and Henri. Henri is my father. I got along well with my Grandma and Yvonne, my aunt. I used to go to Tante Yvonne's on vacation when I was a young child. Yvonne and my Uncle Jean Raynaud had no children. She tried her best to take care of me. She made wonderful French desserts.

My grandma and her daughter Yvonne lived in their family house later in life. It had three stories. My aunt lived on the top floor and she always tried to educate herself, reading many books and learning things my parents did not know. I think she was suffering because Uncle Jean Raynaud was not faithful to her.

Elisabeth's grandparents, Marie and Jean Jamen (sitting), aunt and uncle, Yvonne and Jean Raynaud (center), and father, Henri Jamen (standing behind Jean Jamen)

Uncle Jean built a factory close to Grenoble, where he was working. He loved Jesus, and was always having religious books, or holy water from Lourdes with him. Somehow, I also got along well with him. Later in life I told him about my faith and he always listened very carefully. Unfortunately, he did not have the skill to make his marriage work with my aunt.

After she died, he remarried, to a lady much younger than him. This created a lot of turbulence in our family. Somehow this lady inherited the family house from my grandparents,

Jean and Marie. It was most painful for my father as later in life he was living there, after my parents divorced. This lady tried to restore the old house with many different problems. She could not finish it. Always something seemed to happen: The contractor died, the next one got sick, the third one disappeared, etc.

One summer as I was visiting my hometown, my husband and I did a special ceremony with prayer at the house. We prayed to let go of the house, that no more bad feelings, resentment, grief, will stay there. And I myself would also let go. Of course, I was spiritually attached to it too, as I spent lots of time there with my Grandma and my Aunt Yvonne.

Elisabeth with her father and children at his parents' house in Saint Etienne de Cuines

Family Stories

My great-grandmother Sylvie Humbert Bartholomé was born in 1862 in the Hameau du Vallonnet commune of St. Jean d'Arves in the French Alps. She is also the sister of Michel Humbert, grandfather of my cousins Michele and Renée Humbert. I spent time and vacations with them in the high mountains, where their ancestors lived a life of ruggedness and hardship. Their home is called Auberge des Aiguilles, named after the famous peaks of the mountains.

There it is like wilderness, and so majestic it takes your breath away. Everyone should, once during their lifetime, visit the Vallonnet mountain, 1300 meters higher than where the main village is.

Recently, I have been climbing the steep path up the mountain with Michele and sometimes Renée, sharing our hearts. The joys and the sorrows. If you want to, you can climb all the way to 2300 meters and sleep in the refuge. But you can only go on foot, or with a horse or donkey, or eventually a kind of motor sport mountain bike. Every time we arrive at the Vallonnet I am spellbound. You access it by walking through a river.

Right now, only one couple is living there in the summer. They had enough of the city life and bought a ruined chalet and are restoring it. They want to feel close to nature and the simple life. One night it was raining so hard they could not pass across the river and they were stuck there, in this magnificent beauty, with also a waterfall that charms the nights with its pleasant sound.

My great-grandma Sylvie was not afraid of working hard, especially in the summer in order to go through the winter with enough food.

Sylvie married my great-grandfather from Montaimont, also a village in the Maurienne Valley. They probably met at a fair where they buy and sell cows and sheep. So, she went and lived in my great-grandfather's house by La Perrière in Montaimont. You can also see the house where Jules Bartholomé, my grandfather, was born. It is a very poor, basic and simple village. But it has a view worth one million dollars. When I was a child my mom took me there often to visit our many cousins.

The point I am coming to is this: Despite the million-dollar view, I believe Sylvie was unhappy because her husband became unfaithful. I can feel her sad and heavy heart, and I am deeply sorry about this situation.

I am so very deeply sorry that my great-grandpa could not keep his marriage vows to be faithful. How many bitter tears Sylvie must have shed while keeping track of the cows, making the cheese and butter, and sleeping above the cows on a wooden floor to keep warm, and not being able to have the true love she deserved. In fact, after she died, my great-grandpa married the servant who was working in the farm. So goes the story mom used to tell me. The children also were not able to forgive him, because he put his wife in great agony.

I am myself in the position to repent for all the sins of my past ancestry, that all can be forgiven and receive God's eternal blessing of true love and keep the marriage vows of faithfulness, and that this suffering may never happen again.

Cousin Renée's Tales

Letter written to Elisabeth by her cousin Renée, about their family history

Here is some information about the life of our ancestors and the lifestyle of those generations that went before.

At Montaimont, our original homeland, life was very hard. The earth brought meager resources and did not provide the families' livelihood, because having a large number of children was important.

Even in the middle of the last century, the children from eight to ten years old were traveling on foot, with the supervision of one adult, in the vicinity of Paris, especially Beauvais and Provins. All along the way they were doing their job as "ramoneurs" – cleaning chimneys.

Until 1860, when Savoie was re-attached to France, it was under Sardinian rule, and the little "ramoneurs" would say they were leaving for France.

Concerning our common ancestor, Charles, as well as those of his generation, every year after the harvest he would go to Paris for the winter, and would come back in the spring time to work the fields. This was helping the family to live.

At the beginning, the men would work in the hotels or grooming horses, then as coachmen, and then around 1910 when taxis appeared, they worked as taxi drivers.

Your grandmother Elisabeth had a café-restaurant in Levallois, at 124 rue Fazillan, later called rue Jules Guesde. This café served as a meeting place for the people of

Montaimont, who rediscovered the ambiance of their home village there.

Elisabeth's grandparents, Jules Bartholomé and Elisabeth Milleret, outside their restaurant, with their children from previous marriages, and their dogs

The drivers would work with the taxis for six months each year. They were strong workers who did not hesitate to work long hours, without a break or rest. So, they were easily re-employed from one year to the next.

The big company that hired them was Compagnie 67, which had its headquarters in Levallois. It is from there that in 1914 the famous "Taxis de la Marne" departed, and stopped the Germans in their advance on Paris.

Your grandmother's café was situated a few minutes from Compagnie 67. At her departure, the restaurant was continued by her brother Maxime, then her brother Seraphin, and finally by her brother Daniel until 1938. The restaurant no longer exists as the neighborhood was completely destroyed during renovation.

After the Second World War, life changed a lot. The families were not separated for part of the year anymore, as in the past. The whole family now came to Paris. The children then learned their job, first as "écailler" – the one who works at opening the oyster shells in a fancy restaurant – then manual work or in an office.

This way of life was that of my parents. Since their marriage they were living in Levallois, Paris, and we were born there, all four of us: Robert, Suzanne, Renée and André.

The mountain was abandoned little by little, and now you can count on your fingers the number of farmers with new modern equipment. However, since a few years, some have sought to profit from the new winter sports resort near Saint Francois and became ski instructors.

At the time of our parents, just at the end of the last century, there were schools in all the villages. For example, in Les Mottes, your grandmother's village, there were about 20 or 30 students. Now all the schools are closed and the few children who still live there are picked up by a bus to go to a bigger school.

All the people of Montaimont remained faithful to their village and come back every year for their vacation.

With affection,

Renée Milleret

Her Life Was not a Peaceful River

When my mother, Odette Bartholomé (Jamen), was entering her old age, she reunited her children and grandchildren for Christmas. We arrived by car from Vienna, where we had already celebrated Christmas with Dietrich's family.

I always loved arriving back in my mountains of Savoie. The air there is fresh, the mountains familiar, every single place I know by heart. Here is the place where my grandfather lived, next where my grandmother lived. The other side, my great-grandma, and the ancestors of my father.

Elisabeth's mother with her grandchildren, at the Christmas reunion

The reunion was held at my grandparents' former home in La Chambre, as were all the other numerous reunions. This year my sister-in-law, Marie Josée, one of the best cooks I know, had prepared escargots with garlic and parsley, and other delicacies. There were already all kinds of treats, chocolates and French pastries on the side table waiting to be savored. And the richly decorated Christmas tree was welcoming all of us. We also brought some new spirit from America.

For our Christmas gift this year my mom had prepared something very special: a monetary gift for each one of her descendants, and a letter for each of us that she wrote with her best handwriting, even if it was a bit shaky.

I still remember every word of her letter and feeling her heart of love and sorrow.

She was mentioning her life not being a peaceful river, but because of her dad she could go on and survive. Her own mother passed when she was only 13, and her dad was very busy with the farm, so somehow the neighbor family helped in raising her. Then there was the war and all the suffering which came with it. There was a scene that she repeated often, how one day the Germans came and helped themselves and carried the pigs away. She also had a painful divorce from my father.

Still, she was the driving force of the family and the tribe. Always taking care of people, inviting them for dinner, snacks and coffee. Rendering many services to each one, near to her and further away. She was always helping and giving a heart of love. When she passed, I wrote a poem to honor her, "Parce que c'est ma mère" ("Because it's my mother").

She shed many tears during her life and I am very sorry. It did not help when I joined the Unification Church and moved to America. With the leftist media raging with no understanding at that time, how painful it must have been for her.

But this day was a joyful day, she gave out what she had, forgetting how hard she had worked, and even though her life had not been a tranquil river, today she had her children's families here with her for Christmas. Descendants of love, with each one of us trying to bring fruits of love and multiplying them for the sake of the world.

I love you mom. Thank you.

Elisabeth's mother with her beautiful peonies

Parce que c'est ma mère

Beautiful mother
Mère de vie
Mère d'amour
Mère de coeur
    de bonté
    de tendresse
Mère généreuse
Mère pour tous
    C'est ma mère

Petite mère
Grand'mère
Belle mère
Belle dame
    très digne
Grande dame
Super Mom
    Beautiful mother

Mère de passion
Mère très aimée
Grand'mère adorée
Mère précieuse
    Un trèsor de mère
Mère pour tous
    Parce que
    c'est ma mère
    Beautiful mother

Because it's my mother

Beautiful mother
Mother of life
Mother of love
Mother of heart
    of goodness
    of tenderness
Generous
Mother for all
    It's my mother

Little mother
Grandmother
Mother-in-law
Beautiful lady
    Dignified
Great lady
Super Mom
    Beautiful mother

Mother of passion
Mother well loved
Adored grandmother
Precious mother
    Treasured mother
Mother for all
    Because
    it's my mother
    Beautiful mother

Mère de confiance	Mother of trust
Mère de conscience	Mother of conscience
Mère d'authorité	Mother of authority
d'honnêteté	of honesty
de verité	of truth
et justice	and justice
Mère de ses enfants	Mother of her children
C'est ma mère	It's my mother
Beautiful mother	Beautiful mother
Mère de courage	Mother of courage
tenace	of tenacity
Mère Bélier	Mother Aries
fougueuse	spirited
Mère des montagnes	Mother of mountains
de lumiere	of light
du tonnere	of thunder
et des éclairs	of lightning
Mère du ciel	Mother of heaven
des étoiles	of the stars
et firmaments	and firmaments
Mère pour tous	Mother for all
C'est ma mère	It's my mother
Mère de pardon	Mother of pardon
de renouveau	of renewal
réconciliante	reconciling
unifiante	unifying
Mère d'un monde	Mother of a world
d'amour	of love
vrai mère	true mother
Mère de tous	Mother for all
C'est ma mère	It's my mother
Beautiful mother!	Beautiful mother!

A Teenager's Dream

When I was thirteen or fourteen my favorite movie was (and still is) "Sissi."

It is the story of Elisabeth and Franz Joseph, Emperor and Empress of the Austrian-Hungarian empire. There were three movies. The first "Sissi" is about how she grew up in Bavaria, Southern Germany, among nature and animals and a loving family of many brothers and sisters. Her father instilled in her a love for nature and simple things.

"Sissi - The Young Empress" is about her life in the castle of Schönbrunn in Vienna, a magnificent place with parks so huge it takes hours to walk everywhere. It was difficult for her to conform to the rules of the empire, and especially her mother-in-law, Sophie. But it was a love marriage, and we enjoy seeing the relationship full of attention and care between the spouses in the middle of so many duties.

The third movie, "Sissi - Fateful Years of an Empress" is about her destiny and how she and her prince had to solve many problems between the nations, while keeping their love alive. So it was in the movies.

It was just then that movies were starting to be in color. Before that you needed to be content with black and white.

I liked this movie because it was such a romantic and beautiful love story. And the heroes had to fulfill their responsibility as king and queen, and later as emperor and empress. The music was classical Austrian waltzes, and more, which could make a teenager dream big and high.

Little did I ever imagine at that time that my true love would also come from Austria.

Recently, I walked again in the Schönbrunn Castle, remembering my teenage years when I was thinking how beautiful to find true love. My auntie Trudy had invited me for lunch where she still lives, just minutes from the castle. This was the house of Dietrich's great-grandparents.

Andreas Hofer Haus, restaurant and inn belonging to Dietrich's great-grandparents, named after the Austrian patriot who led the Tyrolean Rebellion against the French

They used to have a restaurant and an inn adjacent to the house, with tables inside and outside in the garden, Austrian style. And Katarina, his great-grandmother, always made a lot of goulash as she was originally from Hungary. Their youngest son, Michael, was my husband's grandfather. The great-grandfather took care of the inn. The great-grandmother made the goulashes, and the elder daughter was responsible for the register.

Dietrich's great-grandmother, Katarina Kokosh, with her husband Franz Stechauer, and family. Dietrich's grandfather, Michael, is standing on the right.

Many times with Oma, Dietrich's mom, we would go to the castle because so many of her favorite restaurants were there. With the view over Vienna and the castle, she would fit perfectly in the countryside. Even at 97 she is an Austrian beauty, behaving like a queen with perfect manners and contentment.

So, my teenage dream somehow became reality. I fell in love with the most amazing man from Austria, and he too fell in love with me. What else shall I want?

Early Years in the Unification Movement

Here we learn how Elisabeth's life changed course dramatically. She went from being forbidden to visit the church in her hometown by her father, to meeting and joining the Unification Church, the new religious movement founded by Reverend Sun Myung Moon.

She was first introduced to the Unification teachings, the "Divine Principle" (DP) while working in Italy as a tourist guide. When the missionaries there left, Elisabeth found a way to reconnect with the movement in Paris. There she was taught this new revelation by the first missionary to France, Reiner Vincenz, a German. The first entries in this section reveal Elisabeth's excitement at hearing this "new truth" and her dedication to the young movement.

A large part of this section contains her journal entries, from the time she arrived in the United States to support the growing movement there, followed by her years in Canada with her husband, where she gave birth to her two children.

There is much emotion expressed in all these writings, particularly great excitement and high spirit at being an early follower of Reverend Moon, and the joy and anticipation of an arranged marriage to a person of a different culture.

The reader should realize that Elisabeth's journal entries were not written with the idea that they would be widely read outside the membership of the Unification Movement. Indeed, it is a precious gift that she has made them public. To better understand their meaning, it is important that the reader be introduced to some basic terminology, as well as a brief overview of the significant events taking place during this time period.

The organization itself has been known by a variety of names. The official name when founded in Korea in 1954 is translated as the "Holy Spirit Association for the Unification of World Christianity" (HSA-UWC), indicating that it was never intended to be a separate denomination but rather a unifying organization. Nevertheless, the rather unwieldy name was routinely shortened to the "Unification Church." Early members in the West often avoided the use of the term "Church," preferring to be known as the "Unified Family," or something similar. In more recent times the organization changed its name to the "Family Federation for World Peace and Unification," stressing the importance of the family in achieving the goal of a peaceful world under God.

Unification Church members regard Reverend and Mrs. Moon with great reverence, referring to them as True Parents, individually as Father Moon and Mother Moon, True Father and True Mother, or simply as Father and Mother. They often refer to the movement as the "Family" and to each other as "brothers and sisters." The member who introduces a person to the movement is known as their "spiritual parent" (or "spiritual mother" or "spiritual father"). In this way, the membership is viewed as an extended spiritual family, with Reverend and Mrs. Moon as the original spiritual parents, and God as the ultimate Heavenly Parent.

Several of Elisabeth's entries consist of letters, written to God or copies of letters sent to other members. It was common practice among Unificationists to end letters "In the Name of Our True Parents," or something similar ("In Their Precious Names," "In Their Names," and so forth). These endings were often abbreviated ITPN, or ITN.

Marriage in the Unification Movement is regarded as much more than a wedding ceremony. It is a sacred, holy union, and a sacrament, an instrument of salvation and healing whereby the foundation for God's original love, life and lineage is reestablished. Through the Holy Marriage Blessing the couple is restored to God's lineage and can establish a "Blessed Family" with children born directly into God's lineage ("Blessed Children"). Before participating in a "Blessing" ceremony, in which large numbers of couples receive a holy blessing on their marriage, the couples drink sacramental "holy wine" to cleanse their lineage. The Blessing ceremony itself includes sprinkling of "holy water," the recitation of vows, and the exchange of rings. This is followed by a period of continued celibacy, a purification time to offer the marriage to God.

During his lifetime, Reverend Moon acted as a matchmaker, often bringing together representatives of different nations to hasten the process of creating a one-world family of peace. Elisabeth met her husband, Dietrich, through this process. It was love at first sight! Which then deepened over the years into an eternal, sacred bond.

During the period covered in this section, 1970 through 1984, Reverend and Mrs. Moon visited France while Elisabeth was there. Still a young member, Elisabeth was deeply moved by this first experience of meeting Father and Mother Moon. It was such a momentous event that she wrote a long article about this short visit!

Shortly after that visit to France, Reverend and Mrs. Moon and their family moved to the United States. Reverend Moon traveled the country, giving public speeches in every state. The most significant events were held in 1974 at Madison Square Garden in New York City, and in 1976 at Yankee Stadium in New York in June, and at Washington Monument in Washington DC in September. Elisabeth arrived in New York to participate in the Yankee Stadium rally.

In that same year, the *News World* daily newspaper was established. Missionaries in the New York area were asked to deliver the newspapers and gain subscriptions from those living in their "Home Church" areas.

This Home Church mission involved each member taking spiritual responsibility for an area of 360 homes, serving and bringing God's love to those families.

It was while serving her families in this way that Elisabeth's spiritual daughter, Christiane Coste, lost her life. She was recognized by Reverend Moon as the first Unificationist martyr in America. Several of Elisabeth's journal entries refer to Christiane and her tragic death.

The Moon family took up residence in the Belvedere Estate in Tarrytown, New York. Reverend Moon often spoke to the membership gathered there on Sunday mornings, or in the Grand Ballroom of the New Yorker Hotel, often called the World Mission Center. Elisabeth attended these meetings on a regular basis. Belvedere is also the location of Elisabeth and Dietrich's Matching and Holy Wine ceremony, while the New Yorker is where their Holy Marriage Blessing ceremony took place.

Also, during this time, membership in the Unification Church in the West increased dramatically. This led to greater public opposition, and parents feared for the wellbeing of their adult children who had joined the movement. Finally, in a move that many religious leaders regarded as a threat to religious freedom, Reverend Moon was arrested and indicted on charges of tax evasion. This led to his being sentenced, in 1982, to 18 months in prison. He served 13 months in Danbury Correctional Institution before being released for good behavior.

For more details on the historical development of the Unification Movement in America, the reader is encouraged to read *Forty Years in America: An Intimate History of the Unification Movement, 1959-1999* by Michael L. Mickler (2000).

For a deeper understanding of Unification theology, the reader is encouraged to read *Unification Insights into Marriage and Family: The Writings of Dietrich F. Seidel* (2016), which contains Dietrich Seidel's autobiography as well as theological and practical reflections on marriage from a

Unification viewpoint. Study of *Exposition of the Divine Principle* (1996) is also recommended.

For additional understanding of Elisabeth's developing relationship with her husband, Dietrich, the volume of letters they wrote to each other, *Beloveds Forever Together: Letters of Eternal Love* (2017), is highly recommended.

Becoming a Member of the Unification Church

December 31, 1970

I was in the Place de l'étoile, looking for the street that connected with Rue le Sueur where the Unification Church headquarters was located. The taxi cab that drove me from the night club where I was with a group of Italian tourists – I was working as a tourist guide – dropped me by the Place de l'étoile.

I knew it was a very providential night for me, and I had promised Reiner Vincenz, the first missionary to France, I would be at the center by midnight to start the first day of the New Year with the family.

By now I did not remember how to get there. The 12 avenues were so confusing, but I felt God for the first time by my side. I was kind of joyful and full of expectation. Going down the avenues I felt like dancing in the streets. I made a few spins around and told the few people on my way, "It is going to be God's Day." Sometimes in Paris, when the mood is right, you can say such things and people's hearts become intuitive and sensitive.

It was a beautiful night full of anticipation on my way to the center. When I finally arrived at my destination and rang the bell a couple of minutes before midnight, having run for a while, I was breathless. I realized the way I was dressed was a little different from the people at the center. I wore a long black dress and I smelled of smoke from the cigarettes and champagne at the nightclub.

But this was a providential night, as I was going to start anew to greet the New Year with God. Reiner told me, "You must take a shower before you can enter the prayer room. You have one minute!"

After the pledge to God, the prayer, I knew this was going to be something special in front of me. I felt like I was representing many French women of the past, present and future, and given a tremendous task to become a new kind of woman.

In my past I had lived an impure life and could feel how much I represented fallen Eve. So, all the loves in my life will now be God first. I felt a true and real enthusiasm, and God as my friend, understanding me deep in my heart. At that moment I think I became a member of the Unification Church.

Sometimes the most fallen people can make a drastic change in their life. One of the first things I remember doing after that experience is that I went to the nightclub where I used to go dancing all night, and there I put up posters for *Pionniers Du Nouvel Age* (New Age Pioneers).

Then I liked to go to the cafés in the Latin Quarter and boldly ask the young people sitting there if they would like to join us at our table, as we were having a discussion about a new age coming. Parisians always like to talk, so they would easily join our table and we would have many lively discussions. At that time, we were inexperienced in teaching Divine Principle and guiding people spiritually, so probably we missed many good opportunities to convince people.

I soon came to understand that our way is first of all the way of indemnity.[5] By paying back bit by bit, condition after

---

[5] In Unification teaching it is understood that, due to the Fall of Man, all people lost their original position and relationship with God. In order to

condition, we could make our way back to God and open the road for many of our French brothers and sisters.

---

restore a lost position, a sacrificial condition of restitution must be made. The making of such conditions of restitution is called "indemnity."

My Experiences with Our True Parents in Paris

A shorter version of this article was published in *The Way of the World*, June 1972

True Parents arrived in Paris on April 2, at noon, and left on April 5, 1972.

On Sunday at 11:30 am, Reiner telephoned from the airport: Our Master's[6] plane is already here. Genie (Kagawa) and Thérèse (Heitzinger) came running to the sisters' room shouting: Master is here, Master is here!

We were praying and jumped to our feet thinking that Master and our Mother were already in the hall. Then Thérèse went to the window to check when the black Citroën with our True Parents would arrive.

We all gathered in the hall, holding our breath. Suddenly, Thérèse said: Here they are. She flew to the door to open it. We heard steps on the stairs. My heart was in my throat, jumping with the noise of a waterfall.

The door opened and everyone bowed, oriental style. I did not dare to stand back up as many of my brothers and sisters did not stand up. My emotions were very strong. Then I saw Master from the back going toward his room. Mother was wearing brown pants and jacket. On our Parents' door

---

[6] In the early years of the Unification Movement, Reverend Moon was referred to as "Teacher" or "Master," reflecting the respect of his Korean followers. Later, he introduced the term "True Parents."

there was a "Fleur de lys" (ancient emblem of a king in France).

A little more than a year ago, in Milano, was the first time I was shown a picture of the Master. I called him Sun Myung Moon. I cried and I started to love him. Today I was meeting him, and my heart was calling him Father.

Master came out of his room again to enter the meeting room. We were waiting in silence and bowed again. Still I did not see the face of Master yet.

We received our Parents with Oriental reverence. As I was bowing, I heard his step and I recognized him. It was my Father coming home after a long absence. Then I saw his shoes: wide, strong, majestic, so stable on the ground.

Master went to the meeting room for lunch. The sun lit the room and his face appeared suntanned and handsome. There were pink roses on the table. I saw then our Mother coming out of their bedroom with a yellow golden dress, western style. Her step was light. We were observing our Parents from the brothers' room, just across from the meeting/dining room.

When I saw Master in the long corridor of our center, he looked like a man from the countryside, a farmer. He looked as if he was coming back from the fields with his hands in his pockets. He was waiting. Whoever would have seen him at that moment would have wanted to make him some tea.

He was wearing the slippers I had seen so many times in the closet, waiting for his arrival. I felt happy to see him with slippers on.

After lunch, our Parents decided to go to the Galeries Lafayette, one of the big department stores in Paris. The PA system that day throughout the store was saying non-stop in

French "Every moment something is happening at Galeries Lafayette." It was so true on that occasion. I felt a great joy in following Master and I perceived great warmth and energy.

Colonel Pak asked me how to get a very big cake as it was the birthday of one of the men in Father's party. I went to call Marie France to buy this huge cake and to have it by the evening.

Barbara came back to get me on the ground floor where I was making the telephone call, and we rejoined our Master who was buying shoes for himself and the seven men in the party. Our Master was sitting majestically, new shoes on his feet, like the king of kings. It was sad that the vendors could not recognize him.

Then Master wanted to go to the ladies' department. Someone asked my name and said Master wanted to buy shoes for me as well. I did not know if I should trust my ears, but it was like a dream in the Kingdom of Heaven. The loudspeakers continued to announce endlessly, "A chaque instant il se passe quelque chose aux Galeries Lafayette."

We could not find appropriate shoes, so Master said he wanted to offer us a purse or handbag. As we arrived in the handbag section, Master said, it is better to have shoes. So he gave money to our Mother and we went shopping with our Mother. She was looking for a light dress with short sleeves for the trip to Egypt and India. First, we went to rue St Honoré, then CCC Store, then "Printemps." Mother picked out a summer coat, icy sky blue. Some touch up needed to be done and the salesperson was being rude, but it was amazing how Mother always kept a calm dignity, ignoring the negativity coming to her. Barbara offered this coat to Mother as a gift from the French family.

Then we went back to "Printemps" to choose our shoes, where we met Father again.

We went back to the center at Rue le Sueur for a meal. There is always a lot of agitation when Master is sitting for a meal because the people who are taking care of him want to do their best to serve him.

After a little time, Barbara came to fetch me and said to go to the room because Master wanted to talk to me. As I was taking off my shoes, I was telling myself that I was going to enter the room where the most important person in the whole world, and of the universe was, and I felt very emotional.

As I entered, I made a bow and felt the heavenly atmosphere, pure with flowers everywhere. I experienced a feeling of wellbeing and in my mind was telling God, "Oh! Heavenly Father!" My Father had an amused smile. Father asked through Mr. Kim what we could visit in Paris. Finally, the conclusion was to go on the "bâteaux mouches" on the river Seine, then Versailles, then the top of the Arc de Triomphe.

Reiner and Barbara asked me to accompany our Parents on the sightseeing trips. The next day we went to take the boat. I made a mistake with the number of tickets. I bought 11 instead of 13. Mr. Kim asked me how many tickets I got and then I realized I needed two more. So I rushed to get two more tickets before boarding.

Our Parents observed Paris from the "bâteaux mouches" along the Seine. The sky of the city was grey. Mother was dressed in blue. She had her arm on Father's shoulder. The tourists around looked unreal, like cardboard.

After the boat trip we stopped at the Trocadero with a view of the Eiffel Tower and the holy ground. Then Master wanted to have lunch in a typical French restaurant. Reiner and Barbara asked me to pick one so I rushed to make a phone call to reserve 16 seats. Coming back, already our Parents and Mrs. Choi were going back to the car. Mrs. Choi asked me where I had been. Already our guests were a little frenzied to follow step by step our Parents. It is true that our Master goes so fast that we must be trained to keep up.

We went to the Boulevard St Germain des Prés in the "Quartier Latin," where the students are, and also where the first cathedrals appeared, the different currents of thought, and the revolutions.

At the restaurant, two tables with eight seats each were reserved for us. When Father entered it was like a bright light of love to everyone in the restaurant. People were suddenly coming alive, smiling at him, telling him where to put his coat, etc. Many waiters came around and the atmosphere was very electric.

When Master is sitting down, he is even more amazing than when he is walking. He talks like a father, with so many aspects, courage, will, beauty and love for the world. Do you know the feeling of being at the same table as the Messiah? To know that he has so many plans and projects to save the world? That the time is rushing, that we must hasten to bring the good news and to have at this moment only our eyes to cry. This is what I did.

Out of our church center, Master seemed extremely sad. The more I was looking at him the more I was crying. At the same time, I was running to get the waiters to bring what Master desired.

Father ordered a trout with almonds and salad, then a tart with ice cream on top, and Coca Cola. Somehow there was some confusion in the restaurant kitchen. It felt like everything came out in the wrong order. I started feeling really bad and sorry as only Reiner and I were part of the party from France and I was feeling totally responsible for the mix up of things. Reiner was encouraging me with his look: "Do exactly what I tell you."

When Master is silent, his heart looks so heavy with all the suffering of God and the universe. I looked at him and suddenly big tears started to fall on my plate. Father said to Mrs. Choi to tell me that he liked the food, and my ancestors were crying through me. I did not know if he wanted to comfort me or if he really found the meal really good.

We went out of the restaurant and everybody took pictures. Then we took the road to Versailles.

Father asked that I explain the history of different rooms. He asked a few questions, in particular where was the Treaty of Versailles signed that ended World War I.

Father was walking through the rooms fast, very fast, running like each minute of his life is precious and counts. It was filled with tourists, which made it very difficult for us to follow our Parents. Father was holding Mother's hand, who was holding Mrs. Choi's hand, who was holding my hand in order not to be lost in the crowd of people, and to make sure everyone kept the pace. I was explaining the different rooms of the castle and she translated everything to our Parents. In one room, Master looked with particular attention at a painting illustrating Napoleon and his history.

When we first arrived at the Chapel there was a tour group and a guide was showing the picture on the ceiling of the Return of Christ. Exactly when Father entered, the guide shouted, "Here is the Return of Christ in all his splendor!" I of course translated this to Father. For me Father was exactly how the Messiah should be. He walked like him, talked like him, loved like him. No questions asked. A picture taken by the Château de Versailles with True Parents and their party is now at the history museum in Korea.

When we came back, we stopped at the Arc de Triomphe, where there was an immense line to go to the elevator. So, with my best tour guide smile, I said "VIP, VIP, Please let us through." And they did. Master's face was extremely sad when he was looking over Paris. Then he bent over and saw the family members who had stayed downstairs and were waving at him. He then put on a very tender smile of a father for his new found children. We found the members downstairs and took more pictures.

On Sunday, Master asked for those who were in the family for less than six months. Many members were there less than one month. Master said it was a good sign.

When brothers and sisters seemed tired, Master clapped his hands to take away our sleepiness. He said, "You do not treat me the way I should be treated. I am much more tired than you." We all felt a big emptiness inside. Master saw our dismay and smiled with tenderness.

The last evening was a special evening. Master was tender, a real father, not severe at all. In his eyes we saw so much love. He spoke on different things. We felt so much love from him and for him that we did not want to let him go. So, he stayed a little longer and had something to eat. We were all sitting around him on the floor, sharing these wonderful moments.

I want to thank our Heavenly Father for all these experiences, and thank our True Parents for the love they give to all of their children.

The Shoes My Father Bought

When True Parents visited Paris, they went shopping in Galeries Lafayette, the big department store in Paris. We went to the shoe department where Father bought shoes for everyone. I was on duty to organize True Parents' sightseeing tour and was not expecting to receive shoes, but I was asked to choose a pair as well.

We each showed the shoes we selected to True Parents. They asked me why I did not choose high heels. I responded that we were witnessing every day and those flat ones would be more comfortable.

That same year three of us, Bernadette Bellay, Jacques Dubois, and myself, were sent to Bordeaux in the Southwest of France. I remember witnessing with those special blessed shoes. One evening by a corner of a street, although tired giving out flyers I met Monique Rabat, the beautiful mother of Chris Allen, who as her son has also a beautiful voice, and she made beautiful evenings of song for our guests back then.

Another beautiful young lady I met then was Christiane Coste (coste in Italian means a price to pay), a physicist who was conducting research at the university. Christiane became an ardent witnesser and died in her mission field while giving out newspapers in her area in New York years later. Father honored her when she passed, saying that she will be one of the first persons he wants to meet when he goes to spirit world. He declared her as the first martyr of the Unification Church in America.

Many other people came that year to the center and joined. I always felt my shoes had spiritual power.

Letter to Missionaries

April 24, 1973

Dear Missionaries in Lebanon, Morocco, Monaco and Andorra,

Reiner asked me to keep you up to date with the latest news here in France. First of all, a big hello and lots of love from Reiner, Barbara and the whole French family.

All the different families came to Aulnay on Saturday, April 21, for two days. The main reason was the visit of Mr. David Kim,[7] who is responsible for all the teams in America.

Mr. Kim spoke for most of the afternoon on the subject of One World Crusade (OWC).[8] To bring the world back to God, the OWC has five goals to accomplish: Unity of sciences, politics, economics, religions, and culture, art and education. Master is working with all his energy now to accomplish these goals.

After that, our Master will establish in the United States "Federation for Peace and Unity" that will replace the United Nations. The future of the United States depends on our

---

[7] David S.C. Kim, an early follower of Reverend Moon in Korea, who later became the founding president of the Unification Theological Seminary.

[8] The One World Crusade, later International One World Crusade (IOWC) was formed in the early 1970s to promote the belief that "one world" under God can be achieved based on understanding and application of the Unification Principles. It operated in various countries, including Korea and Japan (Global Team), USA, and European nations, with members traveling in teams to invite people to attend lectures and rallies.

movement. Mr. David Kim said that now they get free articles on OWC in different newspapers, and that is to restore the persecution by the press against our movement in Korea in 1954.

Also, of great importance is the establishment of trinities – prayer by trinity, resolving problems by trinity, and before going to sleep three people speak together about the events of the day.

In the evening, each city presented a song or played piano or flute, followed by questions and answers with Mr. David Kim. Mr. David Kim is like a military commander of the army. He is aggressive, determined, speaks loudly to chase away the evil spirits, and he says that when he arrives at a place Satan is afraid and packs his bags. We shouted "Aboji Mansei"[9] so loud that all the walls shook, it was so powerful. Mr. Kim left the next morning.

The family continued the program, which was to read one more time the history of the Unification Church. Roland explained the passages that were the deepest, and responded to questions. The family has become stronger than it was during our last meeting for God's Day. The members seem more determined and more organized, even though little problems still exist.

Right now, the team is split up in different cities to help people join the family; many are at the conclusion, in Paris we have four important Christians, two sisters (Thérèse and Christiane), a priest (Father Benoit), and a young seminarian who recognized Master (Philippe). This weekend we also had a weekend workshop, including five people from Belgium. All

---

[9] "Mansei" in Korean literally means "ten thousand years." It is equivalent to a cheer of "Long Live Aboji (Father)."

the people from Belgium and France accepted the Principle at the end of this weekend. As you can imagine it was an important and moving weekend.

All the news from America is good. Often our brothers and sisters from Europe tell us how the years 1973 and 1974 are the most crucial in all of human history, and how much they feel that in America.

I would like to send to you with this letter all the strength that Mr. David Kim has left us with, his will, his confidence, and his determination that we will accomplish and win.

With much love,

In their Blessed Name, Elisabeth

Prayer at Town Hall of Paris 5th Arrondissement

November 21, 1975

Heavenly Father

I pray for the great victory of Yankee Stadium. That Father, our True Father, can be known throughout the world. He suffered so much until now. I pray that all nations can accept him and recognize him forever, and that Your name, my God, can be glorified for all eternity.

Father, during all this campaign, protect all Your family in New York, give them much strength and deep faith; protect especially the life of True Parents. They are so much needed in the world. Protect and give Your assistance to the president of the Unification Church in America, Mr. Neil Salonen. He needs all Your support so much. Help also Mr. Kamiyama and Colonel Pak, and Reiner and Barbara Vincenz.

Every day, please my Father, give guidance to Reiner, that he may accomplish completely his great mission, that he can be successful in every task he does for True Parents. Give him divine authority when he meets important people, and when he guides the family. His mission, Father, is so important. Protect him from all attacks. Give him good people and faithful, that they may collaborate with him and help him in accomplishing his mission.

May the town of New York accept True Parents and love him, our True Father. May this town know the divine light and all people be resurrected to the true life.

Father, we pray for all the teams in USA, may all people who compose those teams be the most faithful and obedient, determined to give their life for You.

With deep concern we pray for the "God Bless America" festival, that this festival can be the greatest festival ever seen. That it can be Your glory, that You may take the whole of America. That this country can be directed by no one but You, so that You will find again happiness and joy, also all Your children in the world. They are so unhappy because they are separated from You. They look for the light. May they all see the beautiful light showed by True Parents.

Father, this is a time of great revival for America. Let this country be Your country forever. That communists can never ever invade this country, but let us be able to stop them, and advance forward with Your words of truth. Father, we promise You to work until all this earth can be purified and all evil disappear.

Father, save America to save the world. This is such a beautiful and wonderful country. So large, and with people of heart and open minds. My Father, bless this beautiful country. That this country can accomplish its purpose to serve Korea and the whole world. May Your spirit always inspire the leaders of the nation, especially President Ford, the current president. Bless him, my Father. Oh, my Father, may his heart be noble and high that he can see the value of our True Father Sun Myung Moon. May he accept to see Sun Myung Moon and they may cooperate together for the salvation of this nation and the whole world.

Father, may we be all able as children of Your family to take responsibility for the world. May also this nation of France cooperate for the victory of Yankee Stadium. Father, guide us every day for this purpose. Give all the French family wisdom, heavenly love and intelligence that we may serve other nations to our utmost best. Let us restore France by serving other nations.

Father, we pray from the very bottom of our heart that the mission of Reiner Vincenz, outside of France, and the mission of Henri Blanchard, leading France, can be united as one. May they become one in heart and in spirit in accomplishing their great mission. Father, give guidance to both of them.

Oh, Father may Yankee Stadium be Your victory in this troubled land of America. May we always be united with Your work, Your will and Your heart.

May we be able to comfort You. We will do it my Father.

In the Blessed Name of our True Parents,

Elisabeth

Prayer at Town Hall of Paris 7ᵗʰ Arrondissement

November 21, 1975

My Heavenly Father,

Thank you from the bottom of my heart because I know You, and You are my Father.

There is so much evil on this earth, so many bad things and misery, because our enemy Satan is working so hard in this time of Last Judgment.

Father, You are my only Father, I would like to say to You how much I need You and how much I love You, because You are the most wonderful being in the whole cosmos. Your heart is the pure one, the best one. How much every day we need to be with You in give and take that we can do only right things, think only positive things, act only in Your direction.

Father, what a struggle every day. You know this. Every time we want to be with You, we are pulled to the other side. We must struggle hard, my Father, to become in Your image. But this is a wonderful fight, because by our tears and efforts we will establish Your Kingdom.

Father, I want to ask forgiveness for all mistakes, all bad thinking. When I have not enough confidence and faith, when I do not work hard enough for True Parents in this so important time. Father, I pray to You that I can become a better representative of You, a person who can speak of You much better, but not only speak, but act like You.

Father, our hearts are fallen and sometimes we act in an evil way. Father, forgive us, and let us be able to be an instrument for You, that the restoration can be successful completely.

Father, I know how great is our responsibility. Father, I want to do better for You, because I feel sometimes You have so few people working for You and understanding You.

Father, I pray for all my brothers and sisters, especially those in positions of responsibility. For the ones who are struggling so much every day to bring Your love and direction in their center. Father, bless all of them. Father every day they are thinking of You and loving You, even if they don't tell You this. They love You and they need You really so much. Without You they cannot act. Father, we pray to be united all together that Satan can never interfere because we are one.

Father, this is good to know that You are here, working with me and speaking with me. Father, I pray to be Your instrument. Please use me to make Your truth known everywhere, to each person I meet. Father, I pray that I can change my attitude and my heart to a better one. Also, my understanding and my reason to a better one that I can serve You to the utmost best, my Father.

You have so few people, my Father, for now and I feel so much on my shoulders to help You and all my brothers and sisters.

Father, I pray for France, that this nation can serve the other nations and the world. I pray for all the political men that they can be people of right heart and spirit. Father, may these people understand Your son, and respect him. Let us be good ambassadors for him, everywhere we go.

Father, thank you from the very bottom of my heart.

In the Name of our Beloved True Parents,

Elisabeth

Prayer on the Way to Charles de Gaulle Airport

Written when Elisabeth was going to the airport to meet members arriving from other countries

December 5, 1975

Heavenly Father,

Deeply in our heart we think of You and beloved True Parents. May Your spirit come to this nation and move this nation upside down.

Father, give us Your guidance to fulfill our responsibility. May we always look for unity and love for mankind. May we always look for what You want and what is Your desire.

Father, all Your children of the Global Team came back to Europe. This is such an event for this nation because Your spirit is with them and You love them so much.

Father, thank you from the very bottom of my heart for True Parents, True Father and True Mother. They are reflecting so much Your image and beautiful heart. They are like You for this. We feel so happy when we are with them.

May we accomplish great things for Yankee Stadium. May we be determined.

Please, my Father, guide Reiner Vincenz to accomplish his great mission in America. Give him always guidance and wisdom and good health. Give him possibilities to accomplish the desires of True Parents.

Father bless America! The world can be saved and Your children come back to You. Father, we pray that also France can be ready to help America, especially for the great event of Yankee Stadium. May we know Your guidance always and follow You. May we save so many spiritual children and go to America to save this nation. Father, we pray deep in our heart for this nation which can save the whole world.

Father, may True Parents receive love from mankind now because they are Your representatives on earth.

Father, we pray for each member of IOWC, for the Global Team and the European Team, that we may melt together as one family as true brothers and sisters. May we love other nations more than our own. The world must be our nation. How beautiful is each nation Father! How they are expressing Your heart deeply.

Father, bless these members from France with all members of Europe, that we will unite together to save Europe and make a United Europe. May we work hard for this, my Father.

Father, bless all Austrian and Italian members arriving tonight.

In the Name of our Beloved True Parents

About Christiane Coste

I remember the first time I saw her in Bordeaux, in the south of France, she was skinny, smiling, with black curly hair, and her glasses gave her the seriousness of a graduate student from the University of Bordeaux. At that time, she was working on research with rats and mice, and sometimes I would visit her in her laboratory. She was always right to the point and very direct in her approach.

We were three people living in the center and I taught her Divine Principle. Rather, we would read together the first French version of the Divine Principle, pausing after each paragraph and I would answer her questions. At first, she could not believe in the existence of Satan. So she had to ask plenty of questions. She would come regularly each week and our study would go deeper and deeper. She understood pretty quickly all the other chapters, but not Satan.

Finally, one day she came to the center and said that she now believed in the existence of evil because last week she was doubting the existence of God so only Satan could let that happen to her. Also, she understood Divine Principle was the truth because she said I was always very calm answering her questions. A little bit more than a year ago I had joined the family. Christiane must have joined about the beginning of the summer in 1972.

Her first day of witnessing was by the beach near Bordeaux. We had a microphone announcing our lectures in the evening and we were singing to attract people. Our voices and our songs were really terrible, but we had faith.

Right from the beginning Christiane showed me so much respect, gratitude and love. One night she told me, once she "adopts" a person her link is very deep and profound. I did not know what to do with all this because at that time I felt still so young in the family and had not yet discovered how to guide and have give and take with spiritual children. I could feel Christiane was such a unique person with a strong personality and sharp mind.

Before leaving for America in 1973, she wrote her testimony and said how much she owed to her spiritual mother, because through her she could discover God. I did not know I could make someone discover God. She gave me so much support and confidence. She never saw my weak points, she only had admiration which forced me to become the person she was seeing in me.

I stayed in the Paris headquarters working as a secretary for three years while she was traveling around the world with the One World Crusade. We wrote each other regularly. Once she sent me a full box of literature, pamphlets and souvenirs to keep for history. I could feel this was so precious for her. Again, she said I was the person she trusted the most so I should take care of that precious literature and keep them in a good place. I put the box with the French documents for history.

In 1976 I came to America for the Yankee Stadium rally and we could meet again.

Journal Entries 1976 – 1978 in New York

The journal entries in this section are from the period after Elisabeth arrived in the United States in 1976, working with early members in New York City.

These writings express beautifully the hope and excitement of the relatively early times in the Unification movement in America. Anyone who has wondered about the life of the "Moonies" in those days will be amazed at the depth of faith and dedication expressed here. The earliest entries capture the life of an unmarried member, working on the campaigns and receiving guidance from Reverend Moon at numerous Morning Services attended by members in the New York area.

Elisabeth writes about preparation for the Matching and Blessing, two of the most significant events in the life of first generation Unificationists. Reverend Moon personally introduced prospective marriage candidates, often people who had never met before and were from different countries. In the case of Elisabeth, her future spouse, Dietrich, was a student at the Unification Theological Seminary in Barrytown, New York, and their first meeting was when Reverend Moon introduced them. Descriptions of their first meetings, the Matching and Blessing ceremonies, and their early times as a couple reveal her faith in God and her willingness to open her heart to this handsome young theology student from Austria, a country that was only recently the enemy of her beloved France.

The final entry is about her spiritual daughter Christiane Coste, who died tragically while carrying out her mission in New York. Elisabeth had already left to join her husband in Canada, where she received a telephone call with the sad news.

MAY 25, 1976

Islandic Airlines - Lux - N. York

Heavenly Father, This is such an historical day going to America for yankee stadium the most important date for you - Heavenly Father may we be able to represent you everywhere we go; live with you all the time. Heavenly Father may we know deep in our heart how to serve you and how to serve our Beloved True Parents.

First entry in this journal

June 8, 1976: *America – Land that We Love*

The day I was supposed to be going back to France, Reiner Vincenz said I should stay here in America. Christiane came at night and brought a beautiful card, "Land that we love," and a postcard showing New York. I felt deep in my heart much love for this city. How shall we love a country, a city? How shall we bring back God in the hearts of men and women? I will learn to love New York more than any other city because God tries to come back here.

The night of the Yankee Stadium rally I will never forget the beautiful heart and spirit of my Father Sun Myung Moon. I never saw before such dignity and strength. Before the official starting, one hour before, there was such pain in the hearts of brothers and sisters because the TV showed negative images of Yankee Stadium. Some seats were not yet occupied, so it was terribly painful.

But all the children of God were united with True Parents, singing and determined to go over the difficulty. God could take this internal victory, because of unity and faith.

True Father was as beautiful as God. His spirit was shining all over Yankee Stadium. This was such an historical day.

Today, June 8th, I started a new job. Jean Pierre and Beatrice try their utmost to give much life and kindness to everyone. In the morning I felt heavy spiritually so I had to try hard to connect with God.

I should learn how to be always high spiritually, with good thoughts, and loving each person I meet. Love is the greatest power. How to be a better instrument to let God's love pass through me.

At 6 pm I went to the Church Headquarters to search for some pictures for the French Headquarters. In the PR office was a sign:

LET'S GO OVER

WASHINGTON MONUMENT

I had to restore relationships with the public affairs staff, because the first time I met them they were so cold. So, I prayed to God to show me their true heart. They were good to me.

I think when somebody is distant, I should pray that we have a better heart to love each nation. We should try to break through any barriers. I pray tonight, my God You can show me the heart of the Japanese, and I will think how to serve them.

June 14, 1976: About the Kingdom of God

Today was such a struggle. I had the feeling I was not even five minutes with God. Why? I should definitely start the day better with spiritual discipline. As soon as I get up, I must search through prayer how to find spiritual strength and send away all negativity.

Yesterday we went to Belvedere. Father and Mother came from the Holy Ground hand in hand, also with some of the children. Mother had a beautiful pink dress. They were really divine, coming from the hill toward the training center where the members were waiting for them.

Father is so dignified. He has so much "allure" knowing he is the beloved son of God, in my heart I felt deep respect and true love, wanting to bow in front of him.

He spoke to us about the Kingdom of God. In order to be entitled to the Kingdom of God we must become good and righteous.

Waiting for Jean Pierre in the late morning with Beatrice and Jean Fred, we met Reverend Ahn (one of the 36 Couples[10]) who is responsible for Europe. He has such a wonderful heart, giving love all the time. He was in front of the main house and called me from a distance. He was surprised that I was still in America.

Tonight, I pray to God to become good and righteous and lead many people to the Kingdom of God. Also, I pray for God to clean my heart, to be His daughter.

June 15, 1976: The Power of Positive Thoughts

This morning Mr. Aidan Barry gave a very deep message. He said God and Father could not feel joy with the 80 percent victory of Yankee Stadium. Nor could we. Since the first of June his heart was aching. Especially western members must wake up and bring victory for the Washington Monument rally.

In the office today, I tried to know the heart and personality of Beatrice, Allan and Jean Pierre. I must feel a connection with them in order to work better together. In fact, sometimes I do struggle to have to deal with typing and invoices. This feeling of starting all over again came, and I did

---

[10] The earliest Holy Marriage Blessings took place in 1960 and 1961, with a total of 36 Korean couples participating. These are considered the elders of the Unification Movement, and are highly respected by the members.

not work with all my heart. So, I will change this attitude and be happy in all situations.

Tonight, I went to the World Mission Forum office and met with Christiane and Jean Fred. We ate together and had a deep conversation.

Jean Fred explained about Mrs. Choi, wife of Mr. Choi who was the first missionary to Japan, how she was always positive with such a lovely smile. Mrs. Choi said that she is a very critical person so she keeps everything inside of her. She does not want to express it, because if we speak criticism it brings a negative spirit. Together, we also spoke about the force of positive thoughts and being always positive. Father does not have any give and take with negativity.

Heavenly Father, I pray to You tonight to become a positive person, not only a critical person, and where I see negativity, I want to stay positive and high spiritually.

June 27, 1976: The Most Important Thing is Love

Today was a great day. Father spoke about the Will of God. We receive so much love from him. I always wonder why he leaves so quickly. I feel like I want to stay longer in Belvedere, or go fishing with him.

Jean Pierre suggested to me to go and visit New York City in the afternoon. So, I met Christiane first at 43rd Street Headquarters. We had lunch together. I felt she was tired. I love her very much. We feel very close together as spiritual mother and spiritual child.

We went with Rachel and Jacques Dubois. Christiane and Jean Fred decided to bring an African lady with us to the Statue of Liberty, but finally they did not come, or we could not find them.

The three of us had a wonderful talk. We spoke so much about our beloved True Parents. How Father educates us each day to become representatives of God and True Parents. This morning he said how much he loved America when he first came. We spoke also about our spiritual parents and spiritual children. Jacques was the first spiritual child of Rachel. We decided also to pray strongly for Charlene who has been kidnapped by her parents.

Then we went back to the center by subway to 43rd Street. There, while waiting for Rachel's guest who did not come, Rachel and I spoke very deeply about what Father is teaching us.

Father explained that when he was on the boat the sea was in such turmoil as never before that one of his daughters came to him and said, "Father, are we going to die?" Father said, "No, just believe in me." Looking at his child he could think of us.

Also, Mother said that every day he is thinking of us so much. He wakes up even during the night and thinks of us. Even his own children could be jealous of his love for us.

Father also spoke to leaders saying that the most important thing is love. We must love our members and protect them from evil. As Abel we must win Cain with love. If not, we cannot say we are in the Abel position.

Don't be judgmental. Father likes this good point about Mr. Kamiyama. He asks Father forgiveness for the members with faults.

Rachel said that in Korea the most important is the reality of internal feeling.

Father also said when members leave, we must cry for them. Father himself feels this is his own fault when one member leaves the family.

June 29, 1976: A New Heart for Spiritual Children

These days I have been so much longing for spiritual children – for such a long time I did not find any.

Coming back from work I had 30 minutes before the lecture at 7 pm. It was so spiritual. I saw a young man on the opposite side of the street. I crossed at the light and walked toward him, and then changed direction and crossed the road with him. I just told him to come to the meeting, and he came.

This kind of miracle Heavenly Father always gives to me. I was so grateful. His name is Bernard. He is German and has been in America for three days. He has a deep heart and believes in God. He said he will change his plans and come back tomorrow to the lecture, and maybe to Barrytown.

I pray to You God, that You take care of him tonight and make up his mind to come to the weekend workshop and prepare his heart to receive Your guidance. Father please be with him and bless him. May he know Your love and will.

Through finding spiritual children we feel reborn with a new heart.

July 3, 1976: Education of the Heart

Today some of us moved to a new house in New Jersey. We had started to love the New Yorker Hotel[11] so much, and also being with wonderful brothers and sisters.

Each day we must look for God, and know what He wants to tell us.

I read in one letter that the most important was the Messiah, the Divine Principle, and the love between brothers and sisters. But each day also we must restore relationships. Education of heart. Positive must become stronger, love should dominate every negative position and we must win all situations with a pure and loving heart.

We need God's help.

May we all tonight prepare our hearts to meet True Parents tomorrow.

July 12, 1976: God Loves Me

Alan and I came back to live in the New Yorker Hotel. Jean Pierre said it will be better to live in the hotel since we are working in New York.

July 4th Father gave a very serious speech. He asked us not to sleep, and at the end he asked who was sleeping. Reiner explained tonight the importance of July 4th – Yankee Stadium was the formation stage on June 1st, July 4th is the

---

[11] At this time, many single members were living in rooms in the New Yorker Hotel.

stage of growth, and Washington Monument on September 18th will be the completion stage.[12]

Today I received a new desk and finally started to set up the office. This afternoon I could feel the joy of God, and see God in my brothers and sisters. I am wondering why since I have been in America I am receiving so much?

Also, True Parents are so near to each one of us. God loves me and He is showing me His love through many of my brothers and sisters.

Sometimes I feel so surprised. Each Sunday Father is speaking about the Blessing. He said that he will match many beautiful handsome Americans with small, ugly Japanese, etc. He wants to prepare our hearts that we may be able to have true love to give out.

May we be able every day to bring God with us everywhere we go. Thank you, Heavenly Father.

July 16, 1976: The Husband God Will Choose for Me

The beginning of the day was a struggle. Satan is still so strong. I am thinking of the husband God will choose for me, and for this how much we must be so pure, faithful, and keep such a great respect for the person God will choose.

May we all come closer to God.

---

[12] In Unification teaching the development of all living beings is described as going through three stages: formation, growth and completion. A similar analysis can be applied to the steps towards achieving a goal.

July 20, 1976: True Mother's Inner Peace and Prayers

Some days ago, we went to the top of the World Trade Center. I hardly saw anything as beautiful as the view over the sea and the city we had from the top. We admired especially the Statue of Liberty and the bridge gate to the world. Such a wonderful place to pray for the world and businessmen of New York City.

The meetings at night with Mr. Vincenz are very inspiring. Such willpower and perseverance he has!

One sister tonight at the meeting spoke about True Mother and the birth of Sun Jin nim. Father did not come right away to the hospital but phoned and Mother said to him, "Please continue to fish; I know how important it is for you to be on the sea." Father caught two tunas very easily. The sister said Mother had such an inner peace and calm. She said also that Mother prays a lot for the members and looks for the education of each child and good organization of the house.

July 24, 1976: Heavenly Heart

On the way of going back to God we should fight every day in order to attend with a heavenly heart. Every day God inspires me and teaches me how much I should love America and American people.

Today at lunch time we ate sandwiches near the Rockefeller Center. Jets of water and a view of the New York buildings, and blue sky. In a way we could find New York romantic! I can imagine how beautiful this country would be if it could run back quickly to God. Even in the work of business or beauty, or art, we must never forget the heart of Heavenly Father and the seriousness of the world's situation.

Tomorrow is a new day, a new week. May we do the will of True Parents always this week and may God bless the work we do for Him.

Father said that he loves America as nobody else does. This means he loves this country as God does. I do really want to try harder to serve this country and understand how Father loves America.

Once I would like to go fishing with Father and see how much I am afraid of the big storms of the ocean, because I heard everybody who goes fishing is so ill.

October 3, 1976: Washington Monument

Father spoke to us this morning at Belvedere. It was a deep, deep experience. Since the 18th of September when I wake up in the morning, I think that Washington Monument was a complete victory. And my heart becomes full of joy and thankfulness. God, dearest God, it was a victory.

Father, when he spoke at Washington Monument, was the most powerful man one could see. How great and dignified he was when he came up to the stage with the sound of music from the Go World Brass Band. There was applause and acclamation by thousands and thousands of people. Dearest Father, you were with God, and God was truly there speaking through you. How beautiful this moment was! How blessed were all the people there!

This morning Father spoke to us and declared that our goal was to liberate Communism and go to Moscow.

He showed his heart and pain and joy. He loved us.

November 27, 1976: To Be Like True Parents

Soon I will have been six years in the family. To be a member of the Unification Church means we should be like True Parents. I am praying to have a new passion in my heart for God and my work as a member of the Unification Church.

Remember God, my first love for You in the streets of Paris. I was running so much on this December 31/January 1, 1971 to find the center in order to celebrate God's Day. I had tears in my eyes out of happiness. The people I asked the way to Rue le Sueur, I told them that was such a great day, and the first day of the year should be dedicated to you, my God. I was reborn and that day was my first love to You, Heavenly Father.

I am looking to God's Day 1977 with great seriousness, in order to pledge again to God my dedication, love for Him and mankind, and start this new year with a new heart.

December 1, 1976: Finding Spiritual Children

Father's speech this morning at Belvedere will be unforgettable. He judged us very severely. "How can we take everything for granted? How as members of the Unification Church can we celebrate our birthday if we have not accomplished?"

At one pointed he asked who has more than five spiritual children. A few members raised their hands (I did), five or six inside the garage.[13] Then Father pointed to me and asked me

---

[13] Reverend Moon spoke in a lecture hall that was a converted garage at the Belvedere Estate. The large doors were kept open and the audience often overflowed outside onto the driveway.

how many years I had been in the church. I answered, six years. He smiled. I bowed to him, and sat again.

His topic was "Self-reflection." He urged us to find spiritual children. At least 3, then 12, and then 84. In my lifetime we must at least find 84 spiritual children. He urged us to become so serious about our mission because the next year will be such an important year, full of events.

Mrs. Choi translated, wearing a beautiful long green dress. Mother came, went, and came back. She was beautiful as ever, perhaps some deep seriousness to go with Father's topic. Father spoke until 11 o'clock, from 6 o'clock in the morning.

Thank you, Heavenly Father. We are so grateful to you.

December 13, 1976: I Met God

Last Sunday, December 5, I prayed to God to save my life. I had known already for a certain time that an accident could happen to me. Also, I did not like to think of how the lifeline on my hand was broken. Then I sang a song to my Heavenly Father, "Grace of the Holy Garden" (I am pledging in my heart of heart, Father my life is for you).

On Monday December 6, an accident happened to me. A car came to me as I was crossing the street (35th Street) and knocked me to the ground and ran over me. At that moment I heard the people shouting. Under the car I met God. I told Him, I cried to Him, "Heavenly Father, Heavenly Father my life is for you, I want to give my life for you." At that moment I even expected to go to the spirit world.

But I stayed conscious despite the pain in my left arm and the whole shock. In the middle of the road I continued to pray, searching to understand what was going to happen to me. I was moved to the side of the road where two ladies comforted me while waiting for the ambulance to come. For me, it was God speaking through them. One said to me, "Jesus is with you." The other one had a deeper heart. She said, "I saw it all. God was with you. God saved your life. God loves you so much. Don't you know that you are the child of God?" I was deeply grateful to God to comfort me so much in this difficult moment.

I stayed in the hospital for three days. The same day another brother had a broken arm too, the right one. In the hospital I could meet Dr. Bergman. Reiner and Barbara Vincenz also came and gave me a lot of support. It was so good to meet members of the Unification Church.

I came back to the World Mission Center knowing that God gave me life. I know in my heart of hearts that my life is for Him. So, with much seriousness I should prepare for God's Day 1977. I am so indebted to God. I pray to enter my seventh year in the family with a new passion for God, a new understanding, a new heart, a renewed dedication.

My Heavenly Father, may we be able as members of the Unification Church to accomplish our mission, and realize the pledge we give to You each Sunday morning.

December 24, 1976: True Parents Are Shining

Two days ago, as we went for dinner, we felt Father was in the World Mission Center. Farideh and I went quickly into the hall. Father was already at the door. He turned back, and we bowed to him. He was wearing glasses and looked like a doctor.

The next day Alan saw Mother and Mrs. Choi, probably going shopping. He said that Mother was laughing and had just cut her hair very short, but so beautiful.

True Parents are shining all over New York.

December 26, 1976: Christmas with True Parents

We celebrated Christmas Day with our True Parents. Father said that also it was the celebration of the opening of the Manhattan Center.

At night there was a beautiful celebration with the New Hope Singers International, the Go World Brass Band, and others. We could see for the first time the film of Washington Monument. Father and Mother and all their family were in the balcony. They were presented to the guests as Reverend and Mrs. Moon. They were smiling and happy. At the end of the night the children went to sing on the stage and then chose the winning tickets and distributed gifts.

My ticket was one of the winners. Kook Jin nim dropped a gift (cookies) in my hands. He walked to me with a such a beautiful heart and gave me the gift. I could grasp it with luck because of my broken arm in a cast!

Thank you, Heavenly Father.

December 28, 1976: Comfort Brothers and Sisters

Heavenly Father,

We pray to You tonight Father to thank you. I thank you for taking care of all brothers and sisters, especially the ones in Communist countries. Father they have such a special mission. Be with them all the time and comfort them.

Soon, Father, we will enter God's Day and 1977. May we purify our hearts in order to start this new year closest to You. We repent for all the things we did wrong in this year, so many Father. Our impure hearts have been so ugly and selfish Father and now we want to change in order for you to use us as Your instruments. May we bring peace wherever we go and Your truth, and Your love.

Father show me tomorrow morning which brother or which sister to comfort, and through him or her I want to comfort You. Thank you, Father, I like sometimes to speak to You so directly. Dear Father you saved my life the other day. I did not know that You could love me so much. I want to learn how I should love You.

In the Most Beloved Name of our Parents, for my Heavenly Father.

December 31, 1976: God's Day, 1977

Father, my heart is so grateful to you that six years ago you led me toward the Unification Church in France where I could attend God's Day 1971. Father, thank you for having guided me during all these years.

Father, the time You waited was so long to be loved by man, and to love him. He could not love You and could not receive Your love. How painful it was in Your heart, my dearest Father.

Dear Father this is going to be the first day of 1977, Your day. May You be happy and joyful today. I want to give You a gift, Father. I do not know how. I will think how.

Father for 1977 I want to promise You at least three spiritual children whatever my mission is, and to become a real public servant. Public servant to America and the world.

Public servant to my brothers and sisters. To have a pure heart.

Father, Happy God's Day 1977.

In the Name of our most Beloved True Parents.

January 25, 1977: To Love Any Person

Today I was busy all day preparing to send books, letters, publications and some gifts to the French members, as Pierre was going back to Paris and could take them with him.

This morning service was very inspiring. A Japanese brother read his writing about the Blessing and how wonderful was his wife. She was the one he always dreamed of when he was still in Junior High School. His feelings were very deep.

Tonight, I am thinking about the Blessing too, and all the surprises Heavenly Father will have for us. Am I able to love any nation, any race, any person Father will choose for me?

February 4, 1977: Rumors of a Blessing

To Silvia

Since a week I wanted to write to you about True Parents' visit and share some feelings with you and Cheryl.

As soon as we saw the car arrive, and True Parents were inside, we greeted them with Korean bows. Some members were waiting in the hall. Passing by, Mother looked at my arm and asked, "What happened?" (I had a big cast from the car accident.)

In the meeting room they said something personal to some members. To Toshiko-san Father said, "When we do beautiful things our heart also becomes beautiful." Father said to Dina, "Why are you here, you are such a good witnesser, you should be in the field." Then, True Parents asked, are you French? Are you American? Trying to guess who is from where.

Then Mother looking at me said, "You are French." Then Father asked me a question which I did not understand. Mother repeated it, "How old are you?" I looked at Father and said, "I am 31, Father," and bowed. Father said something in Korean and Mother looked at me again laughing with an air of complicity. Col. Han translated, saying that Father was worrying about me. Mr. Kamiyama said, "I wish members could understand Father's heart. Father feels responsible for members over 30, especially the ones who have been a long time in the family, and he is sorry that they could not receive the Blessing yet."

Then, as they went out, Father asked Kaomi, "Why are you so small?" and smiled. As they were walking through the hallway Mother once put her arm around Father's waist. When they reached the door, Father turned and said, "I have to go now." So, we said, "Bye bye Father! Bye bye Mother!" Dina said, "Please Father come back," and Sandy said, "Thank you so much Father," as they were walking out.

These were just my personal views and impressions of Father and Mother's visit. But Silvia, what Father said to me it was also for you. It is like you were there too.

What else to say. There are so many rumors as always. Many people try to read Father's mind. Lucille heard from a Japanese sister (Japanese sisters always seem to know many things about Father's plans) that True Parents intended to make a Blessing for older members.

But please, these are only rumors. So, Silvia this is in case, so that you do not get such a big surprise in case it is true.

With my deep love, In their Names, Elisabeth

February 9, 1977: We Feel Happy and Protected when True Parents Are Around

Ulla said just now that True Parents were in the Manhattan Center. Maybe they will come to their apartment on the 30th floor of the World Mission Center. We feel so happy and protected when True Parents are around.

When I came back from work, I met Genie. She spoke about the evening with Father and Mother yesterday with the couples from the 1800 Blessing.[14] Father knows his members so well. He said the moment of the matching is the peak of the presence of God. Genie said how important it is to have complete faith in Father. Father knows exactly who is the best husband or wife for you.

February 16, 1977: My Life of Sins Passed Away

To Heavenly Father

It is like my life of sins passed away. The memories are being cleaned off. I do not know any more the person I was before, as my stained robe is being washed and the clear water of Your love has purified year by year my sinful and bitter heart.

---

[14] The Holy Marriage Blessing for 1800 couples was held in Korea on February 8, 1975. Unification members from 25 nations participated.

Father, what You went through during the whole course of history is so much. I can understand only a little bit of Your suffering heart. Dear Father, Your wonderful purpose of creation, the ideal family, was destroyed by Satan and he dominated us, Your children, for thousands of years. But Father, the light of Your son came to me.

How can I be grateful enough? How can I be faithful enough? My life of darkness has been pushed away, and brightness and warmth came into my heart of hearts.

I changed my robe, Father, to walk Your path. Father, my life is for You. I have no right to have a single desire for myself.

I am sorry Father to have caused You suffering. I rebel sometimes against Your will because Satan tries so hard to keep his ties with me.

But Father it is like my life of sins already passed away. You are going to give us rebirth. Father, I waited for rebirth. It is so long to remain in the death of sins. This morning these six years in the Unification Church looked like 6,000 years. I felt as old as You. For this, I said before, I can understand just a little bit of You, of Your heart. Your son, Father, is the one to really know You.

I feel I would like to write many letters to You. And You would answer back to me?

Please Father look after and care for the ones who need You the most. Don't worry about us. We will make it.

February 18, 1977: The Matching

It was February 17th, 1977. For God it was the last day of the year 1976, as the lunar calendar starts on the 18th this month.

We went to Belvedere to meet True Parents. On the way God showed His beauty through the creation. It was after 5 pm and the sunshine did not want to go. Father, Your sky was so beautiful, You felt so happy.

We went to the main house in Belvedere. Right away Father started to match people. He started with Michael Runyon. Father asked Michael Runyon with which nationality he wanted to be Blessed. Michael said, with a Japanese. Then Father picked a Japanese sister for him.

When Father asked Dietrich Seidel to stand up, he said to him: "Now you are going to be a Ph.D., so would you prefer a wife with much knowledge and who knows everything about books, or rather one with a good personality?" Dietrich answered, "With a good personality." Father was just beside me and he turned to me and pointed with his finger to go out and speak together. I did not realize so much as I even did not notice Dietrich, I could not see his face. Father looked so sure. Then we went to the dining room to speak.

When for the first time I looked at the face of Dietrich, I could see God in his eyes. He was like someone I knew the heart of, and he seemed to know me so well. He was so clear. Both intelligence and warm heart. I liked him so much. I was so surprised that he seemed to like me so much too. We said a few words, like our name and the country we came from. Then Dietrich took my hand and said, "I think I like you." I answered, "Me too." Then we went and bowed to True Parents.

He is from Austria. It seems to be the most beautiful country in Europe. After the matching we talked and talked.

Father chose ten couples and we had the engagement ceremony. We kept our hands on top of each other while Father was praying. It was a very deep moment. I felt so much unity with Dietrich and True Parents. After the prayer we could shake hands with True Parents. The hand of Father was warm and strong. Mother's hand was so soft and giving.

Today, so many people congratulated me because they knew Dietrich. They said so many good things about him. Everybody seems to like him so much.

Tonight, when I went to pray there was so much peace and happiness in my heart.

March 4, 1977: The Blessing

On Sunday, in the Belvedere main house, the celebration of the Holy Wine ceremony took place. We arrived there by car from the World Mission Center, together with Shawn from Ireland and Traudl from Austria. It was snowing that day and everything was white. Dietrich was rather calm but Traudl and I were mostly nervous. I tried to get the atmosphere of quietness coming from Dietrich, but there were too many emotions going on in my heart.

Father and Mother had on their beautiful white robes as they came into the room. Heaven came down too. Father gave some indications about the meaning of the wine ceremony,[15] and then started right away. Colonel Pak, then

---

[15] According to Unification belief, the Holy Wine Ceremony symbolizes the change of lineage, returning from the fallen lineage dominated by Satan to God's original lineage for human beings as His children. By

Mother, then Father passed on the glass of wine to the woman, and the woman to the man. True Parents were just near to us when Kook Jin nim, or maybe his brother, came to me and offered a handful of candies. I told him, "Thank you, not now."

This was the change of blood lineage. We were going back to God's lineage. I bowed deeply to Father. Then he gave me the glass of wine. I noticed his hand gloved in white, a beautiful giving hand. I drank half and passed it to Dietrich. Father was so present, like concentrated or praying for us while we were drinking. Then Dietrich bowed to me and passed back the glass and I gave it back to Father, then Mother, etc. The next couple were Shawn and Traudl.

After the ceremony we received a handkerchief with holy wine. This handkerchief is to be kept from generation to generation.

The next day was the Blessing celebration in the World Mission Center Terrace Room. In the morning we had breakfast and then went to try on our robes. Dietrich waited for me for meals. I was very touched by his attention. He was such a gentleman with good manners. At 12 noon we had a rehearsal, practicing how to walk the 21 steps plus 1 symbolizing the big step in the kingdom.

At 2:30 pm we were in the lobby, with white dresses and the men with dark blue suits. The Go World Brass Band and the New Hope Singers International were singing beautiful songs as we were walking toward True Parents to receive the holy water. I remember the last step we walked toward True

---

accepting the Holy Wine as such a conditional symbol, the couple is grafted into the heavenly lineage, transformed into members of the heavenly family of God.

Parents signifying the Kingdom of God. I felt happiness and both Dietrich and I could feel the fresh holy water on our heads. Then we turned aside and walked back to the entrance. The atmosphere was heavenly and we felt so happy and full of joy.

At night we had a banquet with True Parents in the Terrace Room. All the children were there too. Mother had a beige blouse and red skirt. During the meal Colonel Pak suggested some games, like looking into the eyes of each other (husband and wife). My husband has very deep, beautiful, and loving eyes. After all was finished, we took pictures of each couple with True Parents.

A few days later, on True Parents' Birthday, Father declared this was Day 1 of Year 1 of the Kingdom of God. This was also the most beautiful day of my life until now.

March 16, 1977: Warm Hearts

There is so much warmth in my heart since Heavenly Father blessed us in Holy Matrimony on the 21st of February, 1977. My husband's heart is so deep and warm.

March 22, 1977: A Most Romantic Husband

Dietrich came to New York for four days. He just finished one term at UTS in Barrytown, and before starting the last one he wanted us to spend some time together. Dietrich is a most romantic husband. I already love him very much.

I realize more and more how much our life is for the world. It is to love all people, each person, and our happiness cannot have any value if it is centered on ourselves.

Each day Dietrich and I could speak together. I have a much clearer understanding now of his mission as a student at the Unification Theological Seminary in Barrytown.

I had the feeling Dietrich is longing very much for home, family and children. Sure, this is what all men and women desire. But we are still living in the restoration period and our life belongs to God. I pray tonight that our children will be peacemakers and will serve all mankind much better than we do. That they will love all nations with the deepest heart, know and glorify God and True Parents, that through them the world will become a good place to live.

Dear Heavenly Father, I am most grateful to You that You chose me to be Dietrich's wife. Please Heavenly Father, guide both of us in this new relationship that together we will give out to the world and our love for each other will be so strong that we will be able to do greater things for You, dear Father.

In the Name of Our True Parents.

March 31, 1977: Unity is the Key to Success

This morning Father came to the New Yorker at 6:30 am and happened to walk into the Ballroom where the morning service should have started. No-one knew in advance that Father was coming, but we could imagine that he would speak about a serious matter.

He spoke very long about Communism, the danger for America and the whole world. Then he made teams to save New York. He picked brothers and sisters, and then they received an area to take care of. He said we must feel so responsible for this area, even sleep there and go and eat there if we should eat some place. Father said to believe what he said, even if results are not there right away. Spirit world will work so hard, and God, and we will see results after one year.

Also, he emphasized that unity is the key to success.

Yesterday I received a letter from Dietrich. I was longing for it. He is such a romantic husband!

May 9, 1977: Love Can Cure Everything

Spent this Sunday (yesterday) in Barrytown. I feel a deep love for Dietrich. We arrived there, Mrs. Matsuda and I, Saturday night and spent the night in a beautiful and peaceful room.

On Sunday the morning service was given by Mr. Spurgin on the future of the seminarians. The atmosphere was clean and neat. The students serious, clean cut, with a strong personality. I could feel that Father has a good expectation for each one of them.

In the afternoon we went to drive in the countryside and walk in the mountains with the Matsuda couple. In the morning already, Dietrich and I went for a walk. It was spring and beautiful. For a long time, we could see a deer in the field. She was elegant and fragile. When we walked in the mountains, we felt happiness and joy to be together. We did not talk much, we just felt happy to be together.

As we returned, Dietrich did not feel so well and I became so worried. I did not know what to do. Then I remembered once speaking with Barbara and she said that all men need a mother. So, I felt like a mother to my husband and felt for him such a warm and deep love. I brought him some peppermint tea. While he was drinking it, I felt so close to him. He was really wonderful. I think love can cure everything. It has the deepest power.

I pray to God to be able to love my husband so deeply and this will help to make him a true son of God, an ideal and perfect Adam. Father said recently we must be first a mother, then a bride, then an empress.

I am so grateful to Heavenly Father for the blessing He gave us. Please Heavenly Father, guide us to give everything back to the world and to You.

May 12, 1977: So Grateful

Dear Heavenly Father,

My love for Dietrich became deeper.

I pray to You Heavenly Father to guide me in this new situation in order that our love and strength will go out to the world and reach Your children. That this love will enable us to accomplish better our mission.

I remain so grateful to You, Heavenly Father.

In Their Names,

Elisabeth

May 24, 1977: Saving New York

Tomorrow will be one year since I came to America.

We received a booklet about the Blessing. Reading it I realized more deeply the meaning of Blessing, and restoration.

Today and yesterday I could sell 30 *News World* newspapers in my area. Each time is an experience with God. I start to feel a strong love for my area and people there. Some reject me violently, some others become so curious about Reverend Moon.

Today I read the poem in the *News World* to Joe. He is every day in front of his home when I pass by and his eyes are very bad so he cannot read. I always spend some time also to speak with the carpenter, and people around come by and listen or get excited about Father. They simply can't understand. I feel so serious to show the heart of our Heavenly Father and True Parents when I talk to them. God's heart is wailing desperately for their ancestors and to save the city and the world.

On Saturday, Father spoke at the New Yorker Hotel. It was really strong. I felt bad all day long, it was so much judgement. I realize how much more I have to give out in order to reach Father's expectation.

May 30, 1977: My Handsome Husband

Yesterday, Sunday, was Open House at the Seminary in Barrytown. Dietrich invited me, and Gudrun and I went with her parents. Dietrich waited for us at the train station. He was even more joyful than he used to be. I was discovering again how handsome he was, easily speaking with Mr. and Mrs. Bresh.

I had the feeling I had not seen him for months, and it was like I met him again for the first time. In my heart, while he was driving to the Seminary, I thanked God again. He just told me that we would speak together later, and now he wanted to speak German with Gudrun's parents.

All morning I could not understand a word of what was going on. Only in my heart I felt a deep love for my husband, even if the impression came that I could not communicate with him and reach his heart. The more I was looking at him the more I felt how handsome he is. In my whole life I never met such a person. He surprised me, in a sense. It was not a dream.

In the afternoon we went together for a walk for half an hour. I just did not know what to say. Our conversation was rather dry. Then we stopped by the Gate House where all the children of Blessed Couples are, and we greeted Rosemarie. I am looking at the children now with more interest and new feeling, as soon we will build a family too. It is such a wonder to see all these small kids' expressions of God's love.

Dietrich drove us back to the station. As he was running around to gather all the people who were supposed to go, I quickly wrote a card to him to express my thankfulness for this day. In the car the conversation was in German. I felt disconnected, but happy that Mr. and Mrs. Bresh enjoyed speaking with Dietrich so much. We will have all eternity together, and now this is the time of urgency and restoration.

When he drove us back to the station, again I surprised myself to find out how handsome he was. I was sitting behind and could see his strong shoulders and nice hair, hair cut exactly like I love it to be for him. He looked such a gentleman, distinguished and confident. I was wondering if I was dreaming to have such a husband.

We left very quickly, and on the way back I felt his spirit with me. My heart was at the same time joyful, happy, and painful to go away from him.

Today, Memorial Day, we went for a picnic with New World Forum members and guests. My guest, Eric, was in another car which got lost on the way and they never arrived. Tonight, I felt sadness about this fact. Also, my mind was still with Dietrich and I did not pray enough for Eric. I want to feel more responsible for the mission first. With discipline it is possible to find a good harmony.

Heavenly Father, thank you for the sun, the stars, the mountains, and the huge and wide oceans. Thank you for the love which You created and of which You are the origin. Without You we can never experience true love. May Your heart be comforted completely in the soonest possible time.

In the Name of Our Beloved True Parents.

June 13, 1977: Nobody Came

Today I went to my area early in the afternoon. There were walls and walls to break through. Each person I met, I had to fight to reach their heart. I felt very sensitive too when people did not want the newspaper.

When I went to the Christopher Building, one lady and a young child tried to stop me. She was so excited, calling her friends to stop my actions. I tried to keep love for her in my heart and ask God's forgiveness. Then I turned around the building and started to cry and could not stop for 20 minutes. Today I was looking for one person who could come and comfort me, who could understand God and True Father. But nobody came.

In the Unification Church we experience the highest persecution. But also, we receive the highest love from God and True Parents and husbands and brothers and sisters. Please, Heavenly Father, forgive all these persons who persecuted us. Later they will be so ashamed.

June 16, 1977: Forgive, Love, Unite

Ken McDonald spoke this morning about "Forgive, love, unite." It was very inspiring as right now I feel the need to forgive others who hurt God or even myself. When my heart has been hurt by one person, I think I could not receive a gift from this person. I could not be able to take it. How God, my Heavenly Father, felt during so many bitter experiences He had!

Dear God, I am happy to go out in the rain to sell newspapers with no rain coat, because I know many brothers and sisters in our church are suffering so much still now because they do not have everything they need. Please Heavenly Father, forgive the very ones who persecute us.

June 23, 1977: Persecution and Love

While selling the *News World* newspapers today, one man violently picked up my newspapers and tore them up, throwing them on the floor. He was very angry and shouting. A few minutes later I met Fernando and Heine. They offered me a wonderful coffee and cake. Very deep conversation.

Gudrun went fishing in Barrytown with other different groups from New York. I really want to love my area the most and bring to the people the love of God.

September 5, 1977: The One Who Makes Our Dreams Come True

Tonight, I am thinking about what should be the responsibility of a Blessed Couple. Does Father direct them more directly, and how? Tonight, I feel only True Father could understand my heart. He is the visible God, through him God speaks directly. Tonight, I feel I would like to write to my True Father.

Dear True Father,

Thank you with all my heart for the Blessing you have given Dietrich and myself. Father, you are the one who makes our dreams come true. Thank you very much Father for bringing us the love of God. Without you we are truly in darkness.

True Father, you picked us up from such a miserable situation and you made us to become your sons and daughters. Father, we are so deeply grateful.

Dear Father, you gave me such a wonderful husband. Each day when I think of it, I cannot believe my eyes. Father, he has such a good heart and he is truly your son. Father, I pray to you, True Father, to know my mission and ask your guidance. I feel, Father, to work close to Dietrich in the same field. I feel so responsible for the students in Toronto and their professors. Father, also to support my husband in order that you will be proud of him.

But Father if you think it is not possible for me to go to Canada and work with the Canadian family, which I desire the most, I would like to ask you if it is possible to work with the New World Forum.

Father my heart is so touched when I think of you and True Mother. Our love will always be for you. In Their Names, Elisabeth

October 5, 1977: Dreams of True Parents

This was a dream I had last night.

Some people were gathered around True Parents. The scenes were in color. I sat beside True Father. We had such deep give and take. Not speaking too much. It was more spiritual with feeling. I could see complete understanding in the eyes and expressions of Father. He was like my father, my friend, my husband, my brother, my grandfather, my son.

He said to me, "You can have good conversation with anybody. You are one of the best for conversation."

Then I felt so happy. I felt I was even the same body as True Parents. We held hands together but also our arms were like glued together, like one arm.

Elisabeth holding Father Moon's hand (not a dream!)

We walked in this place which looked like a university campus with fields and buildings. As we walked, I felt I was inseparable from True Father. I could not go away from him because our arms were glued together and love was so strong between us. I felt so much joy and was smiling ear to ear while walking.

Many brothers and sisters were there while we were walking. There was also another person on the other side of Father. I think it was another sister. Brothers and sisters looked at us passing by. It was such a deep experience with True Father as he could understand me perfectly like nobody else.

James told me of his dream on October 4th/5th:

James was with many brothers and sisters in a place like Belvedere. Then he saw True Father coming to me and taking my hand and I had a big smile on my face. Father said, "I like your smile. I remember your smile."

February 28, 1978: Concerning Christiane Coste

Letter not sent to Colonel Pak

This letter is to convey my gratitude to True Father and to you for your comforting words last Sunday morning concerning Christiane Coste. Christiane is my spiritual daughter and I felt such heartbreak when I learned what just happened to her.

We had a very close relationship since she joined the family six years ago. It was so wonderful to have each other and such support. In our friendship we were like mother and daughter, sisters, and sometimes she was like my mother too.

I loved her so much because she was working so hard for God. She herself would always say that she did not do almost anything. Every day she was so persevering and courageous; always honest, faithful and sincere.

Last year she had an operation and was quite sick. As soon as she got out of the hospital she started working as hard as before. She was pale and I was worried for her. I suggested that she rest a few days. She answered me, "How can you tell me that, when True Father after coming out of prison was almost dead and bleeding but still continued?"

Christiane Coste with Elisabeth and Dietrich at their Holy Marriage Blessing

Bernard, my spiritual son, called yesterday and I learned of the blessings Father gave to her and also your encouraging words. I felt comforted and joyful that True Father loves her so much.

In the Name of Our True Parents.

In Canada

This was another time of major transition in Elisabeth's life, both joyful and challenging. She had known Dietrich only a few months when he graduated from UTS and began his doctoral studies at the University of St. Michaels College in Toronto, Canada. Elisabeth wanted to join him in Canada and support him in his academic mission. However, she was not prepared for the major life change of becoming a wife and mother, particularly with a husband who was a graduate student.

She moved to Canada in the fall of 1977. At first, she stayed in the church center in Montreal, visiting Dietrich in Toronto. Then, after she became pregnant with their first child, she joined him in Toronto. There she made great efforts to witness to professors and students, and later ministers, all the while dealing with problems with her health and the responsibility of caring for first one, and then two, young children.

The first entry in this section, "Our Canadian Mission," is a testimony she gave about this period of her life, including many precious details about their situation in Canada. As can be imagined, she was severely challenged. Throughout this time, though, she maintained her steadfast commitment to living with God and to developing her relationship with her beloved Dietrich, who supported her in every way possible. Her journal contains a record of her struggles, together with many heartfelt prayers. The final entry here is a letter she wrote to Reverend Moon in

1985, responding to his request for members to share their life story with him. This letter includes further details on the challenges due to problems with her health, and how she overcame them.

Our Canadian Mission

I remember sharing with Leslie Olivas one Sunday afternoon. Somehow, I felt so close to her because we went through the same pain. Her heart became so beautiful and motherly and deep because of suffering, but she could keep connected with a higher center and not keep any grudge.

I was telling her I do not know how I survived the time when I was pregnant with my first child and very sick. The young center leader seemed not to understand that sometimes pregnant women had nausea and could feel pretty sick. He told me, because I could not follow the schedule, I should not live in the center any more but rather join my husband in Toronto. On the train I cried all the way, telling God not to worry, that I would never leave Him in my heart, even if my body could not function at this time.

So, I joined my husband in Toronto. Dietrich was very helpful in connecting me to the center there. I started part-time, doing first small jobs where I could serve. I remember all those tears while mending the laundry of my brothers and sisters. My heart felt so broken and I felt no value. I really appreciated my husband at this time. He was the mediator for me to connect to the church again, encouraging me and explaining my health condition to the national leader.

Our first child, Christopher, was born in 1978. He was the first Canadian Blessed Child boy born in this country. So, because of him my heart is connected to Canada for all eternity. Two years after, our second child was born – a daughter, Diesa. Father named her because the same day was a birthday celebration at East Garden [16] and UTS President David Kim asked Father to name her. Today, Mother's Day, she gave me a book of poems that she wrote during the year, and a big card where she wrote: "Dear mother, all what I need from you is LOVE."

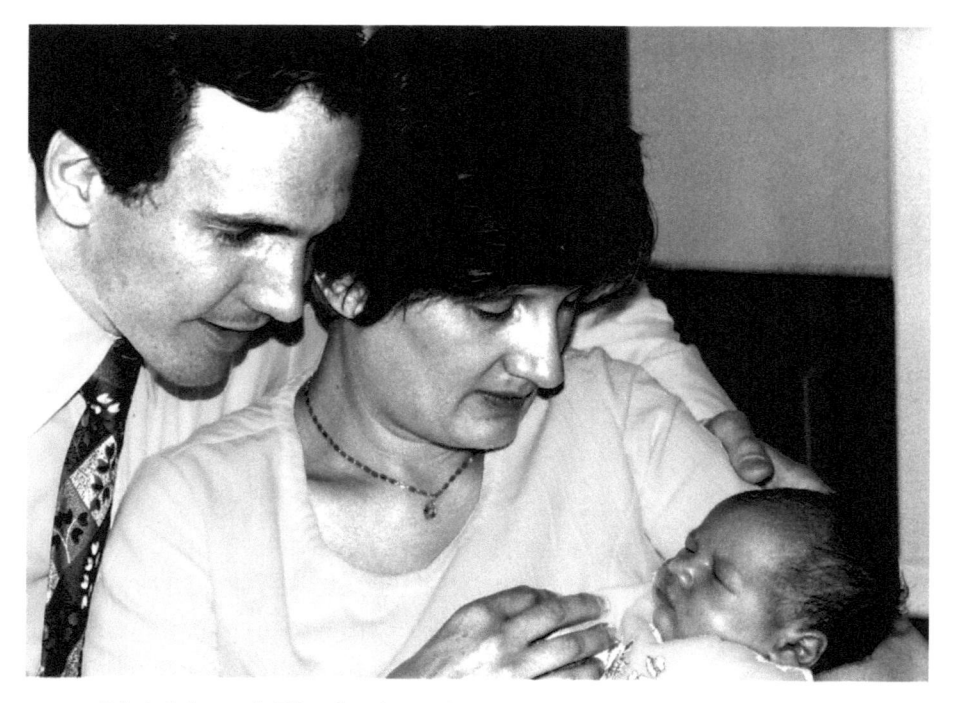

Dietrich and Elisabeth with their infant son, Christopher

Since my children are older now, I have more free time for the mission. But I will always remember those years when Dietrich was studying to get his doctorate in theology and our children were very young. It was truly our time in the desert.

At first, we worked with CARP on the campus organizing many conferences. As not so many Blessed Families were

---

[16] The home of Reverend and Mrs. Moon in Irvington, New York.

around, I shared babysitting with other student families. Some mothers were very good and I felt very confident. Some other times I would feel always anxious that proper care was not given to the children, or not a good atmosphere. But somehow I felt it was important that I make some contribution with a sincere heart, even though I had poor health, and my husband had a hard time to do fundraising and witnessing beside his mission of studying, which was given by Father.

At that time, we were living in the married student building apartments in Toronto University, and it was ideal for Home Church. Across the street was the campus, so it was also ideal to witness to students and professors. I made a point to invite for dinner each professor of the Toronto School of Theology, starting with the Dean, then with the professors my husband had classes with. One by one they came, sometimes with their wife. We cooked for them. They came to our home, so it was easy for them to make the first step toward the Unification Church. One time a famous professor told us because of his position he could not come to the Unification Church right now but he knows very well this is where he will end up.

Then we went to parties for students. We became very well-known everywhere. Every week we also had a pizza dinner in our apartment, where we showed videos about our church and Father's life. At times our living room was almost crowded. So we had a happy problem. It was pretty animated too, so much talk going on about Reverend Moon, I loved it.

A few of those students became professors now and we still keep in contact. Some of them went to New ERA conferences. Also a few Theology professors got into the habit to invite Dietrich every year to give a talk about Unification Theology to their class and show the Blessing movie. One time there were 300 students. There was such a wonderful feeling to be accepted. That evening I had a glimpse of how our future should be, giving talks to large audiences and people responding with sincere hearts. It was so energizing.

Then came the time to visit ministers. We had to move outside Toronto because the prices in the city itself were too high. We were one and a half hours from the Toronto center. Dietrich was now in his last phases of studying, writing his Ph.D. thesis. His topic was "Marriage and Family in the Christian Tradition."

Again, I had problems with my health. I had to go from doctor to doctor. I also have to say that I had three miscarriages, and each time it was such a traumatic experience. Everything seemed to go wrong, my heart, my gallbladder, my stomach, my uterus. I thought I had to overcome death, to face it whatever. I was so weak I could not even walk to the bus station. My husband felt so overwhelmed about what to do because he knew he had to finish his studies no matter what. At the same time, I felt I needed to be with him until I felt better. I could not do it on my own. It was not only the desert; this time it was hell. It is OK to have a good marriage when everything is OK around you, but in very trying situations it requires so much effort, love and sacrifice from the other spouse.

On top of it all, I felt completely isolated from the church center, from the Blessed Families. No one visited me apart from one Korean 777 Blessed Couple.[17] I felt cut off from everyone. I missed my brothers and sisters so much. I really wished someone could visit me. One day in desperation I

---

[17] The Holy Marriage Blessing of 777 couples was conducted in Korea on October 21, 1970. Unification members from ten nations participated.

called my spiritual father, Reiner Vincenz, and told him about my health. I could not even take care of my children. He asked me as the first question, "How is your relationship with the center?" I said OK, but I know it was not ideal. Maybe I did not know how to communicate enough, or connect enough so that I could have the blessing or protection of the spiritual leader there.

Because of the distance, my spiritual father could not practically take care of me, but after the phone call I knew I had to do something. I could not just wait for people to take care of me, because it seemed that at this point everyone was overwhelmed by their own situation. Besides, Father was going to prison, and after seeing the video where Mother was crying, myself I could not even stop crying.

In a situation where I was isolated, cut off from everything, sick, no spiritual life-line, I decided, as my husband said, to "go after it." My husband always reported to President Kim or Dr. Ang almost every month about the progress of his studies and our situation, but because of the distance and being in another country it was not enough. So we had also to connect strongly with the national leader in Canada and center leader in Toronto.

Young center leaders, fresh from the field, do not know how to deal with families with two, three, four or five kids. They really wonder what we are doing all day and why both parents are not on the front-line! Reverend Paul Werner was the new national leader in Canada. I felt I had to start all over from the beginning. The center members were meeting every Sunday night at 5 pm for questions and answers with Reverend Werner, and of course all the families were invited, also for Sunday Service.

The first few times I started going to Sunday Service, I thought I would never get there because there were so many obstacles. First, I had to find a babysitter or leave the children with my husband while he was studying. Then, go on the bus, subway, and street car, all three, one after another for one hour and a half. By the time I arrived at the center I was so exhausted. When we were singing holy songs, I could not stand. I could not sing because it required too much energy. I just sat there and cried. I felt nobody besides God could really understand what I was going through.

The next step was we would go as a family to attend the Sunday Service, or the question and answers. The children were left in the basement of the center with one or two mothers or fathers. I felt quite estranged from young brothers and sisters because I could not be with them. But I had to work out different things. If I cannot go fundraising, do I have no value?

It was the time of visiting ministers. So, while my children were at school (morning only for young children in Canada) I decided to take responsibility for 40 churches in the area where our apartment was located. In between, I was still going to many different doctors and trying everything under the sun, from homeopathic medicine to Chinese herbs to macrobiotic food to acupuncture, etc. Somehow God kept me alive. When everything seemed so dark that I even thought maybe it is easier to die, God popped into my life with a new doctor, a new approach, etc. My challenge was to keep faith no matter what.

The first minister I visited was a Polish minister. Paul Werner's policy was that the members do not need to go in pairs, you go on your own. He said, you should learn to be a pioneer to regenerate yourself. This first minister I visited got so mad at me, shouting and cursing. It was so hard to take.

At this point I could not tackle anything. Everything made me cry.

Anyway, I dragged myself to the ministers' offices, breaking through one barrier after the next. I went to Bible studies. My goal was to visit at least three ministers in their offices every week and talk about Father, and go to one or two Bible studies, and in this way follow up with the minister and congregation. Then I went to the center before the Sunday Service and attended an outreach meeting. Participating in those meetings and doing a minimum, symbolic condition of visiting ministers gave me an opportunity to connect more strongly to the center, making a small offering.

Although my health did not become perfect, it improved. I still have to keep discipline with food and exercise. Then I can manage my health.

Two years ago, Dietrich graduated from the University of St. Michaels College in Toronto, after many hardships and obstacles. He had been teaching in Barrytown already for a few months. As we were packing our luggage into the car to go to Toronto for the graduation ceremony, we heard that there was to be a special meeting with one of the sons of True Parents at the Seminary within an hour. So we unpacked and waited for him. The next morning we headed to Toronto in time for the graduation ceremony.

So now we feel we are very indebted to True Parents and my husband wants to use all his knowledge to become a theologian with heart, and bring the religious and academic world to True Parents. On one of his visits to the Seminary, Father signed Dietrich's thesis. Also, we went to East Garden one time for a celebration and President David Kim introduced us to True Parents. Somehow, he explained to Father that those students who went for doctoral study needed a lot of faith to graduate.

Dietrich dressed for his graduation ceremony in Toronto

This is my testimony to share with other families, emphasizing the absolute necessity to connect with a spiritual leader, or with the church center closest to your home, if you are in a situation where for different reasons you do not have a mission directly connected with our Unification Church. In this way, God's blessing and protection can reach you. Also, sometimes we may feel the church does not take care of us. We should "go after it" ourselves and make good relationships as much as possible.

At one point in our life we may need to have a job outside the church to raise our kids. At this moment it is very important to keep in touch with the church. Make small offerings, tithing, cooking once a week, bring guests to the center to study Divine Principle or to the Sunday Service. Visit ministers, whatever is your talent make an offering to God. If not, we are just like other families. To follow the Messiah requires an outstanding character and tradition of life.

Journal Entries 1980 – 1984

These entries in her journal, beginning in 1980, were written during the time the Seidels lived in Canada. They reflect the challenges faced by many Unificationists as they transitioned from their lives as single or engaged members, living communally and working as missionaries, to married couples with children.

Elisabeth, like other Unificationist wives, struggled with the responsibilities of being wife and mother, giving birth to and raising children, and needing to raise money to support the family home, often while the husband was involved in mission activities. Dietrich was challenged to complete his doctoral studies, participate in seminars organized for scholars on the Unification teachings, and work with the local Unification community; and at the same time support his growing family on little money. Naturally, this was a life of hardship. For Elisabeth, the hardship was intensified both by health issues and by her ardent desire to serve the Unification Movement, a movement that had not yet adjusted to a membership composed of families.

Through all the difficulties and tears, Elisabeth's writings continue to reflect deep gratitude for her life, for the opportunities to serve God and humankind, and her hopes for a better future. They are the words of a true pioneer.

Dear Elisabeth,

   Happy GOD'S DAY 1981.

For your spiritual birthday I wish that you may always feel our Heavenly Father's joy about the coming of His Kingdom. May we both contribute to His joy with all our might in the coming year.

   In the names of our precious True Parents with all my love

         your Dietrich

November 16, 1980: The Origin of Love and Peace

Dear Heavenly Father,

Thank you so very much for creating us. As each Sunday we renew our pledge and our life to you. You are the origin of love and peace, calmness and harmony. Please Father, may we radiate all the goodness that comes from you,

Heavenly Father, my heart is so serious about witnessing to the academic world. You let me meet with so many people. Please Father let us arrange a good set up for our children in order to have free time for witnessing.

Father, be with Dietrich as he started a three-day fast today. Give him strength and energy and specially your inspiration. In Their Names.

November 17, 1980: The Tragedy of the Fall of Man

Dear Heavenly Father,

Your tears, Heavenly Father, were so bitter for so long. You had truly no-one to love You and comfort You. Since the Fall of Man everything became such a tragedy. Father now our True Parents love You with perfect love. For the first time Your own son and daughter are here on earth, opening the way for all of us.

Father, let us be prepared all the time to go through any kind of difficulties with Your heart and the heart of True Parents. May we be able to fulfill all your expectations. Thank you, Heavenly Father, for this day.

I pray in the Name of our Beloved True Parents. Amen.

December, 1981: As you Loved Me, Love one Another

Dearest Heavenly Father,

Thank you for the beautiful Children's Day, 1981. Father, thank you for the end of the 21 years course of our True Parents and the start of our own.

Dear Heavenly Father, I love You. Tears rolled down my cheeks as True Father said, "You went through the desert where you had to follow the command. Now my teaching is: As you love me, love one another. This is how we should live in Canaan."

Dear Heavenly Father, thank you so much for all my beautiful brothers and sisters. This morning of Children's Day 1981, prayers were so deep and tearful. I saw some scars too on my dear brothers and sisters. All of them have been beaten up by Satan to the very bones. But here they were, beautiful brothers and sisters, proud, dignified, shining the light of True Parents. At the same time so humble, so poor, giving out everything as servant of servant.

Heavenly Father, You raised them up from the dead as You raised me up from the dead several times. Father, today I am thinking back to our journey in the desert and I know how suffering Your heart was to let us go into those tribulations as we obeyed the command, with untold suffering.

Father, today I pray for those who made me suffer the most, that those too can have a way to go to Heaven. I pray for the man who, in my first Home Church area, took all my stack of *News World* newspapers and threw some in my face, some into the garbage and some on the road. I pray that spirit world will collaborate with him, that he can repent and attend our True Parents. I pray for the young mother and child who all the time chased me out, calling me names, and who never wanted to let me say one word. I pray, Heavenly Father, that You may truly forgive her and give her one more time the chance to hear Your word.

Please, Father, remember all those who were good to me too, that now they can become true disciples. The beautiful lady in the coffee shop who gave me a drink of Coke in the hot New York summer, and the Greek shoe repair man who bought a *News World* paper every day even though he could not read English. Please, Father, bless them all.

Father, remember Christiane, my spiritual daughter, who gave her life for her Home Church area in Harlem. Heavenly Father, remember her courage and devotion when she died, as she prayed that her death would not be in vain but that True Parents will have success in New York.

Father, remember my car accident. That horrible driver rolling over me in his huge car. I could just babble a prayer to You that my life was for You. You came under the car together with me. I could feel Your warmth and my body was passing exactly between the wheels. Thank you for the lady passing by who said to me while I was waiting for the ambulance, "Do you know you are the child of God?" and the other one who said, "I saw the accident. Jesus saved your life."

And you, Christiane, you took such good care of me afterwards. You were right there at the hospital, then in my room at the New Yorker you washed my hair and cleaned my room, taking so much time out of your busy schedule. Thank you, Heavenly Father, for Your daughter. Father, remember how courageous she was after she herself had a surgical operation. She came back from the hospital and right away she started witnessing. Father, I always remember I said one time to her, "Please Christiane, take care of yourself, take some rest, some vitamins, some good food." And she said, "How can you tell me such a thing, don't you know that after Father came back from prison and was all beaten up he started right away his work for God? How can you tell me, you my spiritual mother, to rest?"

Now, Heavenly Father, let me find spiritual children for Christiane, and continue the work here on earth for her, and may my accomplishments be shared with her. Please, Heavenly Father, accept some accomplishments or good things that I did for her benefit. I pray for her Blessing, Heavenly Father.

Father, I remember the night before the Blessing, Your warm heart and Your care for me. In my heart You told me your dress is going to be washed, all your past is past. My name was not even on the candidates list but I was called a couple of hours before the matching to go to Belvedere. Heavenly Father, I saw Your look, the color of Your eyes, when my future husband looked at me the first time. You had such beautiful compassionate eyes.

Father, thank you for our two beautiful children. May they grow to perfection, serving you with a better heart and deeds than we as parents did.

Father, thank you for raising me up again from the dead after childbirth and two miscarriages. Hospitals are the hell of hell. My body was so weak that I was so open spiritually and could not fight all the fears around me. Father, forgive the doctors who mistreated me, the unhelpful nurse who let me wait too long at home, the sarcastic doctor when I lost my baby, and the one who did not want to see me because it was Sunday. But Father, remember specially the beautiful lady Dr.

Kasari who truly saved my life, who called me every day to encourage me. Her love, strong spirit and exact medicine cured me. Father, remember her good heart eternally and give her many credits and blessings.

Father, don't let any more brothers and sisters go to the hospital unless three others pray for him or her continually. Father, don't let any Blessed sister meet heartless doctors. Please Father, never again. I pray today, Father, that we learn how truly to take care of each other. Please, Heavenly Father, listen to my prayer.

Father, thank you for the beautiful words of True Father, "How now shall we live in Canaan?" Your tears rolled down my cheeks.

Father, I am so sorry how selfish I was. I did not take care of my best friend, Cheryl. Father, she went away but I know her heart, she will come back. Please, Father, forgive her again. I pray that you will give her a chance to come back. Father, she did everything for my country, France, when it was so hard at that time. She was working like a horse and fasting so many times. Her heart was good. Father, she and I love each other.

December 26, 1981: Heavenly Father, Our Parent

My Heavenly Father,

Father, when I saw my own little son suffering and in pain, in my heart I knew Your heart so much. Father, how You must feel like a parent towards each one of us.

Father, many times I felt I cannot see hospitals any more. Please, Father, close my spiritual senses, I am feeling too much suffering. Be with Christopher, Your Blessed son. Heavenly Father, cure him with Your energy and Your love.

May the bump on his head be healed overnight by You. Heavenly Father, make him feel better and completely well by tomorrow.

I pray that he will become a faithful son for You, making a history of goodness. That he will do so much better than we do.

Be with his Daddy, who is in Hawaii for a conference: "God, the Contemporary Discussion."

Father, fill us all with new strength and new energy coming from Your loving and peaceful heart. Father, as a new year is coming up very soon, we pray to be able to purify our hearts and start anew with You and our Beloved True Parents. Please, Father, forgive all our mistakes.

Thank you, Heavenly Father.

I pray in the Beloved Name of Our True Parents. Amen.

December 31, 1981: The Light of Beautiful Canaan

Heavenly Father,

As all these years have gone, we came out of the "desert" holding ourselves strongly to our True Parents. Our victorious True Parents. Father, truly I see the light of beautiful Canaan. It is shining from deep in my heart, reaching my people's heart. It will be a new commencement.

Oh Father, dry the tears of my brothers and sisters. Together with You, Heavenly Father, let us forget and forgive these years of tribulations, suffering, and let us never show again our scars hidden underneath our clothes.

Brothers and sisters, the time is come also for you to dress up as bride and groom. Joy of all joys, the True Children of our True Parents are entering Canaan. This time, Father, we will hold each other's hands so tight that nobody will slip if the road is still icy. Father, I see beautiful lights shining out from the hearts of my brothers and sisters, reaching out to the hearts of their people, becoming True Parents and giving birth to sinless children.

Father, how indebted I am to all my dear brothers and sisters.

In the Name of Our Beloved True Parents. Amen.

HAPPY BIRTHDAY HEAVENLY FATHER

April 20, 1982: *Praying for Christianity*

"Run, Run, Real Man. Run and Run!" How much I am missing True Parents tonight. How many struggles in their life to vindicate You, dear Heavenly Father!

I pray for this evening when many Christians will meet at Anne Benoit's house to hear about "Cults" and deprogramming. How indignant I feel tonight, Heavenly Father. Your own dear son has been so much mistreated, facing so much fundamentalism and narrow-mindedness. I wonder how to move their hearts for You, Heavenly Father, but especially for our True Parents.

Father, make a situation happen tonight where we can truly, truly vindicate our True Father. Give us the love to move their hearts for our True Parents. Speak through our mouths, dear Father.

Purify me, Father, my heart and my tongue, that I can speak Your truth, Father. All of these Christians have been praying to You and to Jesus.

Let me ask tonight a special favor from Jesus of Nazareth, and may he come in person to speak to the heart of the Christians about his mission and his will now. May we all feel Your presence, Heavenly Father.

I pray for Anne, her ancestors and her family. Please, Father, give her many blessings and may we approach her in such a way that she will be able to hear You. Also, may all the ancestors of the others come to them and inspire them for Your will today.

I pray for a pure atmosphere, for Stoyan, Martin, and Dietrich. May they all be your speakers.

"Run and Run, Real Man." I pray for the wellbeing of "Tiger" Park in the spirit world. Father, let us be bold and courageous like him. Let's look for confrontation.

Father, I want to go to St. Michael's College and look for confrontation. Father, let's have another interfaith group.

I pray for Cecile. May she be eager to learn more from You and accept True Parents in her heart. May Martin find the right words to move her heart.

I pray Father that Your special presence may be felt this evening.

In the Name of our True Parents.

June 25, 1982: The Joys and Tears of Fundraising

Yesterday was June 24, Thursday. I went fundraising at Bay/College Mall. First, I met a wonderful lady. Her name is Jacqueline. She bought a picture for $500. We had a brother in the Lord, she said, who feels he has been called to help people, and is he looking for a place to organize a meeting. His name is Manuel. He will call me, she said. Heavenly Father, may your blessings be upon this man and may we be able to work together for You and True Parents.

Then the security guard came to me after I showed my pictures to a few other people. He said I was not allowed to fundraise in the mall. He brought me to the office. I felt very sad and at the same time a tiger inside to continue God's will.

I met a nice lady. She had a good heart and was sorry that fundraising was not allowed. I felt like arguing and was a little upset. Then I could not help but start crying. (We had a tough night, as Diesa woke up so many times during the night and I was more sensitive than usual.) I told her I felt so sad to see some people Godless. Then she started comforting me and said if I would come to her door, she would have bought the picture. I said thank you, and left.

True Father said that until the end of June will be a difficult time for our church. Then there will be resurrection.

I already felt such wonderful things started happening. God is answering even the prayers I had years ago. In the past five years, I went through many physical hardships, car accident (where God saved my life), miscarriages, post-partum problems, etc. Each time I stayed in the hospital I was truly desperate. All the fear spirits were sticking to my body and I felt this is the desert, the long and difficult desert that the Israelites went through. I had no energy to pull my spirit and body together. The doctors were heartless and sarcastic. I felt helpless and called to my brothers and sisters. Everyone was busy, busy walking through the desert. How lonely we must have felt, all of us.

Then I prayed for the doctors, and wrote down my prayers in a diary. I prayed that no one sister will ever meet such doctors again and that heavenly doctors will be raised up.

Recently I could inspire a heavenly doctor, Dr. Jan Kryspin, to write to Reverend Kwak and work for our health clinic in New York. Each time I see him, I feel tears deep inside, tears that we cannot see. And I know that this little prayer from a time of despair was answered by God. Today, I feel how special he is to God and to me.

Dr. Jan Kryspin

June 29, 1982: Dr. Kryspin

Dr. Kryspin just arrived back from New York. He called this morning and was so happy and inspired. He said so many things are happening in New York. He can't even imagine. He went to the celebration in Belvedere for Day of All Things, and he said it was so special. He heard Reverend Moon speak for three hours about creation. We will meet this week together with Stoyan.

Dietrich is in Barrytown to work with the Youth for God tour for a week. I just finished fundraising and will drop by Dr. Kryspin's office.

Today is Diesa's birthday. Precious little girl, two years old. This morning I put my right hand on her head and thanked Heavenly Father. She bowed together with me.

July 14, 1982: "Moonie, No Thank you"

I am waiting for Charla to pick me up to go to the Bible Study. I am waiting in a coffee shop. It is a nice sunny day.

In my heart I am waiting to hear news from Judge Goettel. He is supposed to pronounce the sentence today.[18]

I met a young man who said, "Moonie, no thank you." After my explanation, he said he realized his judgment was one sided.

July 24, 1982: Meetings in our Home

Charla invited me for lunch after the Bible Study. Good talks about marriage and matching in the Unification Church. After the Bible Study, Cathy brought up that the first murder was the one of Jesus. Ann was rather indignant.

---

[18] This refers to Reverend Moon's trial. He was found guilty of tax evasion and sentenced to 18 months in prison, of which he served 13 months in Danbury Correctional Institution.

Yesterday we had a meeting at Stoyan's house, on the topic "In Search of the True Family." A Japanese couple from the toy library came. Also Dolly from Israel and her husband Emmanuel, and Ayub and Stoyan's neighbors. We feel a breakthrough in Home Church activities.

We regularly invite professors and students to our home for talks about Unification Theology, etc. Through our academic contacts many developments are happening here in Toronto.

My health is much better than it was, though I found it is still not possible to fully take care of the children by myself.

Dr. Kryspin is now working three weeks a month in New York with Dr. Bergman, and one week in Toronto. He is teaching his patients Divine Principle as one of the cures for them. His wife is also a medical doctor, and a very wonderful person.

July 30, 1982: I Need God and God Needs Me

Today is a beautiful day. I feel God in my heart. I need God and God needs me.

Dietrich left for Portugal yesterday for a New ERA conference with 300 theologians. He is supposed to give a short presentation about Unification Theology.

This last Sunday John and Stoyan taught Ayub and Cecile at the center. We are beginning to feel more united together now. I know God will help us to make strong unity between home members and the center. On this foundation success will come.

I feel a great love for Canada. This is also my country.

Yesterday night I read in Father's speech: "I have no fear. The way of righteousness is the way where we have to be bold and strong."

Yesterday Cecile jumped into the river to rescue a Portuguese child who was drowning and saved him. Christopher was very excited to tell the story.

It is hard when Dietrich is away. Tears are coming and dropping into my breakfast. I feel myself it is crocodile tears and how some people must be truly lonely. There is such a gigantic work we have to do.

I feel the heart of witnessing today and comforting people. But I have to fundraise today. My bag is heavy and my back hurts. Also, my heart feels pretty weak. This is not a complaint; this is just the way it is. I feel joy in my heart because I feel God. I need God and God needs me. I want to be like Father, have no fear, be bold and strong.

Many times, my mind and my heart are flowing toward my early brothers and sisters in the church, those we met in the early beginning of the church in that country. How many tests they went through and how many tears they shed. Some of them left. I say to myself, Oh God I should have fought with them more strongly and protected them from the enemy. I think of those who have been victorious, who marched into Madison Square Garden on July 1st,[19] and my heart is full of joy.

Today our prayers are so powerful, because so many foundations have been made. If I go to a place and say a prayer, I know that this is spiritual but it will stick in the wall

---

[19] This refers to the Holy Marriage Blessing of 2075 Couples held in Madison Square Garden on July 1, 1982.

and be there to work into the people's hearts, like paint that we cannot remove. I feel a golden age is coming in our church.

I am missing my early brothers and sisters from the church in France. I knew them so well. Their beautiful hearts and, oh God, how much they persevered. I pray for those in Europe that soon they will receive the Blessing. And they will make France a heavenly place.

In Their Names, Elisabeth

August 2, 1982: How to Touch People with a True Heart

Yesterday and today were really difficult with the children. Diesa cried all the time. Sometimes I get very upset and out of patience with her. It is so hard to be a good mother, firm to discipline our children and loving as True Mother.

On Saturday, Stephan, Ayub and Cecile heard a lecture on history given by Gill. Some of us take so long to understand Heavenly Father's heart. Tonight, Stoyan is coming to teach about the mission of Jesus.

Yesterday night Norah Fordham visited. She likes the women's liberation movement and wants to be equal to her husband. Her testimony is full of sadness and without love. How can I touch her with a true heart? How to love the people as True Mother does?

August 31, 1982: Dream of the Kings of France

Yesterday night I had a dream. I was in Paris at the Louvre. I was searching for and finding children's clothes belonging to the kings of France. Each time I held suit or other clothes I prayed for this king in spiritual world.

There was a gold chain bracelet which belonged to Henri IV!

The dream seemed positive for the kings of France!

December 7, 1982: Comfort through the Crickets

Dear Heavenly Father,

You saw me crying so many times today, and You must be sad too. You must feel exhausted as I feel also, but still so many times You comforted me through the singing of a cricket.

We should have already had so many spiritual children work with us and extend the work of our True Parents. But because it is not so, how hard the burden is some days. Yesterday night we were speaking about Joan of Arc and how courageous she was.

In Their Names

February 28, 1983: In the Hands of God

We must put ourselves day after day into the hands of God. Today is the anniversary I think of Christiane Coste's death. May she benefit in spirit world from the good deeds I am able to do here on earth, and we can share everything. I pray that she may find happiness today from upstairs, and she can see coming the Heavenly Kingdom.

I am on my way to give an invitation letter for the 11th of March to the professors at St. Michael's College. Then I will have lunch with the Christian ladies, Ann Benoit and Marti.

Yesterday Dietrich gave the Sunday Service. He had the flu and everything seemed as dry as a split pea.

I am fighting not to feel discouraged or drained out. It is hard. This is why I am remitting myself today completely into the hands of God. He will give me new strength and renew my spirit and I shall walk with my True Parents and witness for them.

He will hasten the Pentecost to come and renew all my brothers and sisters, and comfort their suffering hearts and wounded spirits from all the battles we went through in the wilderness.

Father, may the day of the blessed land of Canaan come soon! Fill my husband's heart with your life and your spirit. Then we can give this energy and life and fire to others. May we harvest the faith of the most faithful Christians, and put ourselves completely in your loving hands.

In Their Names, Amen

March 7, 1983: Making God's Heart Joyful

Sometimes I feel discouraged. But in the end, hope will come.

On Saturday we had toy library in our building and a French lesson. I took the last crackers and cheese and juice for the snack for the children. Dietrich had a few dollars for the shopping for the week. We have no car to do things fast and quickly, to visit people, and no babysitter to trust.

We have Bible Study this evening, and invited people. But we have no presentable couches for people to sit on. My hair looks terrible and on Friday we have a dinner at the center for theologians and ministers. No money to go to the hairdresser. I feel so limited, and we have the most wonderful and powerful message to share.

But Heavenly Father, this is nothing if I could bring a spiritual child to You and make Your heart joyful.

March 10, 1983: *Raising our Children*

Yesterday we went for lunch at JoAnn Thompson's home with the children. When I came back, I felt so exhausted. My children behaved so terribly. I realize they have no discipline or good manners. I felt so terrible and faulted myself as I did not give a proper education to my children as being God's children and Blessed Children. I will have to work on it very consistently.

Seidel family in Canada

After coming back from JoAnn's house, I was really angry with my children and felt so sorry about the situation. At this point our family is very much under stress.

This morning I talked with Mrs. Armstrong, the teacher from the nursery school. She said Christopher and Diesa are so loving toward each other, and warm and embracing. She felt our family is strongly linked toward each other.

She noticed our children do not mingle too much with other children. Also, that Christopher has a very great attention span. He can work and work wholeheartedly on a project or art work without stopping, no matter what happens around him.

She suggested that we do not talk too much to them about good manners or behavior, but that they will follow our example.

She said if children fight together at home, remove them and have a separate room for each to play until they cooperate. Have things ready for them. They can have a corner for themselves and learn to take initiative.

Tomorrow night we invited theologians and students and ministers for a dinner presentation at the center with a talk from Reverend Porter. I pray to find a reliable babysitter.

January 27, 1984: Dream of True Parents

Last night, in my dream, True Parents were coming to Canada today. When they arrived, Mother first sat down in the meeting room. She had long hair with a pony tail and a long dress with dots. I went outside with Christel to pick some strawberries to give to True Parents, the kind from the woods.

Then I passed near Mother in order to go upstairs and prepare the fruit for them. Mother called me and scolded me. She asked how long I was in Canada. I said nine to ten months, and then realized a whole cycle of one year was already accomplished. She said I should smile. I don't remember what else she said but the feeling that remained was I should be positive, and change my attitude.

Then I went upstairs and the strawberries became so small in quantity. I looked for other fruits to make a fruit salad. The other fruits were old and not so good. I felt a very sad feeling. I asked the sisters to please help me make a fruit salad for True Parents. But they were busy. Then I woke up.

Letter to Father Moon

January 1985

Dear Father,

This is my testimony:

I was born in a small French town in the Alps Mountains on October 18, 1945. My mother had me baptized in secret from my father as he was against the religious establishment.

My brother and I grew up in a very tense atmosphere at home since my parents did not get along. So I could not look up to my parents in giving me direction for my life. I was a sensitive child and could not do well at school when the teacher was too authoritarian, but did very well later on when I established good loving relationships with those teachers who had a more round and sensitive personality.

As more fights were going on at home, I centered my life around my school life. When I was in college, I knew I wanted to go around the world and discover something. I wanted to do great things and started to have aspirations. I had a book of sayings and remember writing them down on my exercise books. Especially I felt Confucius had some substance, and I would try to remember and apply his words. My father did not allow me to go to church, so I had no contact with the Bible.

My parents divorced when I was 17, and at that time I decided to start my journey. For seven years I visited, worked and studied in different countries in Europe. My wandering experiences taught me many things about life. During my time traveling in Greece I was very moved by the beauty of creation and started to think about the existence of God. Although I had so many adventurous situations, I never thought that people could be outright evil. When I was in trouble, some mysterious good fortune always seemed to protect me.

When I arrived in Italy, I was looking for God. I was sharing an apartment with a friend and she said she knew a group of people who could answer all my questions. But as she had been a Catholic sister who left the order and I had no religious education she said I would not understand. So she refused to give me the address. (She was studying the Divine Principle but never became a member.) For days and weeks I was thinking about this group, and after much perseverance I got the phone number. When the time came to go to the center, I felt it was a very important time and was extremely joyful. I decided to walk to the place and started running and dancing at the same time. It seems that I just could not wait any longer and God was calling me.

The city was Milano and it was October 1970. When I entered the center, I saw right away a picture of True Father praying. We could not see him well in that picture but I could read below: "I will teach you how to pray." I went a few times to the center there. When Martin Porter had to close down the Milano center, I decided to visit the French family in Paris while I was taking a group of Italian tourists to visit the capital during the Christmas season.

During this stay I could go to the center every day. I was wondering why Reiner was so skinny and everybody else so pale, and why all the members were dressed so old fashioned. How are they going to interest any French people with this rigidity, I thought. But their eyes looked so beautiful. There was shining sunshine inside. And when Reiner opened his mouth to speak it sounded just right. Everything he said sounded true. It sounded extremely deep and extremely serious. It moved my deep inner self. My spirit was so hungry and my heart started beating for God. I was discovering something very precious.

Most of the time Reiner was teaching me personally and pouring out all his heart and soul. Through him I felt God and the compassion of a father, and someone was taking care of me. I had no objections concerning the teachings of the Divine Principle. I had many questions and they were all answered.

I was invited to come for the God's Day celebration on January 1st, 1971. I had an obligation with my work to assist the tourists in a restaurant, but I promised Reiner, I will be at the center before midnight. Quite late I found a taxi which dropped me off at Place de l'Etoile and I could not remember which one of the 12 avenues leads to Rue le Sueur and the French headquarters. After much running I felt again the same joy coming on me when I was going to the Milano center for the first time. I started again running and dancing, and as the people were in a good mood that night I wished them A Happy God's Day 1971! I finally found my way shortly before midnight and arrived at the center when brothers and sisters were entering the prayer room. I accepted True Parents and decided to follow this way of life.

At this time the family had a condition to find new people so that there would be 21 members in the family. As a few people joined about this time, it seemed like a brand-new start. From those 21 members which I remember, about 10 are still in the family now. I love those early brothers and sisters very much. I wish one day I could serve them, take care of them and make them always happy.

In 1971 and 1972 most of the members had a job and we witnessed at night time. There were always people coming to the center and a lot of spiritual activities. I liked witnessing very much and felt very enthusiastic. When one starts speaking the Divine Principle the direct power of God comes, bringing life and hope to God's children.

True Parents came to visit us in February, 1972. I was fortunate to help Reiner arrange for their visit to Paris. They brought us to Galeries Lafayette, and True Parents bought us shoes. I felt these shoes were most special as I would witness with them and they brought me luck and good fortune. At one point I could find 14 spiritual children.

After a while Reiner asked me to be his secretary, and I was in the position of an elder sister to many of my brothers and sisters. I liked Reiner's personality and could unite well with him. It always helped me to grow and overcome difficulties when I could share my heart freely with him. God's presence and support were there when I mediated for my brothers and sisters.

When Reiner and Barbara went for a new mission in the United States in 1973 with some members of the French family, it was a time of trial. Satan tried to shake up the whole tree. Especially the change of leadership brought many tests. Many situations took the last energy out of me and even more, nevertheless at the end I always felt the guiding hand of God. Looking back, I am amazed how I could survive all of these challenges.

It took me a while to understand that every leader is different and brings a different aspect of the True Parents. First, I thought if we do not work exactly as Reiner had instructed us that it was not God's will. At one point I was very confused and I asked two other leaders to pray with me every day at the holy ground. Later on, a deep unity came about with Henri Blanchard and all the leaders.

In 1973, 1974, 1975 members were joining the church. As Henri's secretary, I always felt concern about the well-being of the new members, helping them make decisions to join and getting started on a new mission. Henri was embracing and never judging, and it brought another element into the French family.

In 1976 I went to the United States and worked in a jewelry business. It was a new and beautiful experience to see the True Parents every Sunday at Belvedere. What I liked best was sitting next to my spiritual daughter, Christiane Coste, and the joy of seeing the True Parents was multiplied.

Just before the Blessing in 1977 I had a car accident (in December 1976) where God saved my life. As I was crossing the street a car ran over me, first hitting my back, and my body went under the car between the four wheels. At that moment I shouted to God, "God I want to give my life for you." And I thought I was on my way to spirit world. But, as I was lying there, a lady came to me and said someone went to call the ambulance and she said she saw the accident and that I should not worry because I was a child of God and Jesus saved my life. These words were so beautiful to my ears. I knew as I was passing under the car, I had felt God's presence around me very strongly. I had a broken arm as the main injury, and during my stay at the hospital I witnessed to nurses and doctors.

The Blessing with the 74 couples was another beautiful experience with God. I felt Father was my Father, I had a deep trust in Him and He knows best. Before reporting about my Blessing I would like to share some experiences with my spiritual daughter, Christiane, as she is now in spirit world.

For my recovery at the World Mission Center it was heart-warming to have the support of my spiritual parents and spiritual children. Christiane was visiting me often and I knew how busy she was, but she made it a point that it was very important for her that she could take care of me.

I was always amazed by her personality: persevering, hardworking, and never taking the easy way out. Sometimes we could witness together and she was so single-minded witnessing in the cold winter of New York City, while I always needed some coffee to warm me up.

At one point she had to be hospitalized and she was so happy to see me when she woke up from the anesthesia of the operation. She started working right away after her stay at the hospital and would go at 5 am to Harlem to distribute newspapers, and then go to her work at the Central African Embassy, and do her mission with the New World Forum at night. I told her she needed some rest first, but she said no, because Father, when he came out of prison, he was also very sick but he started his mission right away.

What I liked the best about her was her seriousness for her mission, but also she would somehow always be there when someone needed her. All the little things she did to brighten up my days made her unforgettable.

When she died in Harlem in February, 1978, Father declared her the first martyr of the Unification Church. Now I feel I want to find some spiritual children for her and I pray for her Blessing too.

When Father matched me with my husband, Dietrich, we went to another room to talk. I saw the loving eyes of God through my future husband, Dietrich Seidel. After seven months of separation period, I joined my husband in Canada, where he had started to study for his Ph.D. in Theology.

I joined the Montreal center for a while, and participated in witnessing and fundraising activities. I have to say it was hard as I was pregnant and felt very sick. It was a humbling experience as I was expected to be on top of things and could not live up to these expectations. Then the center director asked me to leave the center as I was of not so much help.

On the train back to Toronto, I cried and comforted God. I was sorry that I could not be active as I used to be, but my heart and faith for True Parents will never change. Then I remembered some brothers and sisters who had been suffering in our church from physical difficulties, and I wished I could do something for them. Dietrich, my husband, was very good in mediating for me to Martin Porter, and I went to the Toronto center working part-time until the birth of our son, Christopher. By then we got an apartment in the student building of the University of Toronto. Because of Dietrich's studies we could witness to many professors and students and invite them to our home to see video tapes followed by discussions.

We had also good experiences doing Home Church in this international student setting, as well as having public talks at the university on topics like "Unification Church, orthodoxy or heresy?" One evening we were discussing with one of the theologians about how God experiences joy and so forth. He told us that at the present time he cannot be a member of the Unification Church, but ultimately he knows this is where he is going to end up.

After the birth of our second child, a daughter, Diesa, I experienced health problems which are still a hindrance for me now. I wish to explain to you, Father, in order to see more clearly how I can overcome it and be more able to work for the mission.

After Diesa's birth I had post-partum problems, and then two miscarriages followed by complications. I don't even like to recall these difficulties because it was a time of great suffering for me. In those times of physical problems, I felt very open spiritually. It was especially difficult when I had to stay at the hospital. I was so weak that I could not pray by myself. I wanted to ask two other sisters to pray for me and support me, but I could not even ask anyone.

Around that time, the Blessed sisters in America were going to CARP, and I was really concerned about what Father was asking from us. I cried for my sisters because I imagined their difficult task to leave their children and follow a team schedule, being more than 30 years of age. I had so much respect for them and deep gratitude for their sacrifice. Somehow, I felt guilty that I could not go, and I did not know how to handle my own situation. At that time, it was very hard even to look after my own children as I was always feeling very weak.

In 1983, I developed irregular heartbeats, and stones in the gallbladder, and my digestive system was not functioning properly. At times it seemed to me that Satan tried to make my body so weak to get at my spirit.

I went to a doctor who knew about western and oriental medicine. He said, when looking on the lines in my hand, that some people have emotional problems to overcome, but I will have to overcome physical problems because my line at one point was so thin that I could even die. But if I overcome, the rest of my life will be strong and healthy. It was like God encouraging me that I will make it. Emotionally it was very demanding to go for tests so often in the doctor's office. Again, I felt so lonely and desperate and could not control the spiritual environment.

For a few months I had to stay almost all the time in bed. I wished to go to visit the center, but had not even the strength to walk to the bus stop. Again, I felt miserable. I wanted to contact ministers and professors but could not. I knew God was very sad. For about three months, I think, I cried every day, not just for my own situation but also for my brothers and sisters, especially the Blessed Families. I wished we could be united strongly in heart. I tried to comfort God because He was the only one who could understand my heart. It was also a time of tension with my husband, as he always felt pressure that he was to finish his study mission as quickly as possible. I know it was also a time of trial for the other Blessed Families and members of our church.

When Father went to Danbury, I realized my own father was in prison and felt like I was in prison myself. I felt very sad when I saw the video tape where True Mother was crying so much. I could not help but cry for three days. Mother said we need to repent and to unite. This is true. Lately, I felt more than ever before that if one of my brothers or sisters – I am speaking now mainly of the Blessed Families in Canada – has difficulties or is unhappy, I feel I am unhappy too. If someone is cut off, I want to bring him back to God and repent. I feel a deep urge to unite on a higher level than before.

Dear Father, for the conclusion of my testimony I want to tell you I will try harder to work for the betterment of our church and for the establishment of God's Kingdom. I am sure there will be a new beginning. Since the end of last year my health is improving and is more stable. I am looking forward to visit ministers and pray with Christians. I feel like a difficult cycle in my life is now over and I want to bring True Parents' spirit with more power, determination and confidence.

In the academic world, I can foresee a bright future. Positive professors regularly invite Dietrich each year to give a presentation on Unification Theology in their classes. The students are not only positive, they welcome us. After the presentation, the professor usually asks us to answer questions together as a couple, and it is a very uplifting experience.

Dr. Jan Kryspin (seated right) with Dr. William Bergman (seated second from left), the Seidels and others at a seminar on health

One medical doctor here in Toronto, Dr. Jan Kryspin, who participated in science conferences and other conferences in our church, runs a clinic together with his wife – also a medical doctor – and would like to have a "Unification Clinic" to unify medicine. He would also like to organize in Canada "The World Medical Health Foundation." He would like very much for a member of our church to work with him. He said he is my spiritual son, so I feel responsible for him. Although I helped him for a while in his clinic, giving some spiritual support to his patients and organizing health seminars etc., I feel someone with medical knowledge would be more appropriate. He is very enthusiastic about contacting medical doctors to do something about the unification of medicine. I believe he and his wife (who also signed the associate membership, but is not as close as he is) have a lot of experience. When the time is right, I pray they will help True Parents' hospital in New York. When Dr. Kryspin came back from the last science conference he said, "It was the best founder's address ever, and Mrs. Moon was so dignified and so exceptional. I understand Reverend Moon cannot be the Messiah without Mrs. Moon."

Dear Father, please be well. We love you and True Mother very much, and we want to show it by our exemplary life and accomplishments.

When we think about your life we are moved to tears. Your suffering will not be in vain, as you planted in our heart the seed of true love. With this powerful weapon, we will go and heal humankind until there will be no more tears, and we will all rejoice in the Kingdom of God forever.

I write all this in the Names of Our True Parents,

Elisabeth Seidel

Later Years in the Unification Movement

This section covers the years near the end of the twentieth century, when the Unification Movement had matured and was entering a time of harvest. A fine account of this period is available in the publication entitled *The Fruits of True Love: The Life Work of Reverend Sun Myung Moon*.

Reverend Moon's trial and imprisonment for tax evasion had not slowed down the work, but had rather energized it. In particular, numerous clergy in America were supportive of Reverend Moon, seeing his plight as a threat to their own religious freedom. Unificationists were excited to finally have common ground with Christian ministers. Reverend Moon stressed that there was no need to convert religious leaders, but rather it was important to work together to raise the moral standard and solve the social problems rampant in secular society.

In a move that surprised many longtime followers, Reverend Moon opened the Holy Marriage Blessing to people of all faiths. Married couples were encouraged to renew their marriage vows, and at the same time receive the Holy Wine and a Blessing on their marriage from Unificationist Blessed Couples. Reverend Moon encouraged the members to educate ministers to be able to officiate at such rededication ceremonies for their own congregation. Elisabeth spent significant time and energy meeting with ministers in the area local to the Unification Theological Seminary, where Dietrich was now a professor of theology.

This was also a time of harvest for the Seminary, with graduates from the early classes returning to take up positions on the faculty and administration, many of whom, like Dietrich, had now obtained a doctorate degree. These included Dr. David Carlson, Dr. Michael Mickler, Dr. Tyler Hendricks, Dr. Keisuke Noda, Dr. Theodore Shimmyo, Dr. Hugh Spurgin, and Dr. Andrew Wilson. Several moved to the local area together with their families, bringing the hope of a new generation of their own Blessed Children as well as the children of Reverend and Mrs. Moon, known as the "True Children," whose visits to the campus are featured in Elisabeth's journal entries.

At this time, the Home Church providence was somewhat transformed into what was called "Tribal Messiahship." Here, the emphasis was not so much on an immediate neighborhood of 360 homes, but rather included the physical family and inhabitants of each member's hometown. Couples were encouraged to return to their hometown with their children, and to serve their own extended family and neighbors, becoming spiritual leaders, or "messiahs," in their own communities. Inspired by this development, Dietrich and Elisabeth spent increasing amounts of time in Europe, both in France and Austria, serving their respective families and communities.

This move brought up the very real difficulty of marriage between families of recent enemy nations. Dietrich's father was a Nazi and his mother Austrian; Elisabeth's family are French, and they suffered greatly during World War II at the hands of Austrians and Germans. To make matters even more challenging, the torrent of unfavorable media coverage against the Unification Church continued longer in Europe than in America. Elisabeth details much of their difficulties in her account of "Reconciliation and Mending of Relationships between France and Austria-Germany in My Own Family."

It seemed like the harvest was still far away in Europe. Indeed, Elisabeth describes facing and overcoming persecution and disappointment, even beyond this period. It took strong faith to continue the journey to realize true love.

At the Pond

Recently Father came twice to UTS, one time in March and another time in April. It is always so wonderful to walk around the campus with him and see him talking informally to couples. He always wonders why there are so many children around when we should be moving out to our Home Church areas. Father always gives out money to be shared among the children.

Also, he sat for about an hour at the pond and asked some brothers and sisters to sing. It was a time for everyone to feel especially close to True Parents.

A few days ago, a sister seminary graduate came here to give her testimony. Her husband is now a state leader and she was sharing how she felt one of her missions was to minister to families. She was saying something like this: There were six or seven members in the center on the front-line full time, and about 70 families living in the area. It seemed to her that those seven members were carrying all the burden of the front-line, and it was such a difficult task to have families connect and participate according to the degree of their ability. Even to come for Sunday Service at the center was a big event.

This seems to be a problem in all nations and for me as well. There are resentments and hurt which need to be healed, but we should free ourselves from those chains and move forward.

Visits to Ministers, Spring 1989

After visiting about 40 ministers in their offices, and sometimes paying several visits to the same minister, my conclusion is that those ministers are ready to cooperate in the providence if we do our utmost best.

My talks with them were always very direct and to the point: About Father Moon, the Unification Church and the Seminary. I would approach the ministers by saying that my husband is teaching theology at UTS. A few of them came to visit the Seminary and shared a meal with us.

In the spring, a Catholic priest came for dinner at our home. He said that during this visit he had the most intense theological discussion in years. When we asked him about his ecumenical meetings, and which church he felt closest to, he replied that it is our Seminary.

I feel that in the area close to the Seminary there are more ministers who are ready to work with us.

In the city of Hudson also, I made good contacts with ministers. Some of them remembered our students visiting them a long time ago. One Catholic priest said he will never forget this sister who visited his church regularly on Sundays. She used to wait for a long time in the bitter cold of winter for the shuttle to pick her up.

Moreover, I went a few times with Kate Jones to monthly Christian Women's meetings in Hudson. Kate is well known and well-liked by those ladies. There are between 100 and 200 Christian women from different denominations who meet regularly.

Dietrich giving the flag of the Family Federation for World Peace and Unification to Father Godé, a local priest

Therefore, I feel that every tear, indemnity or loving care will not be in vain. I pray that Christianity will unite with the Lord of the Second Advent.

Journal Entries 1988 – 1990

The journal entries in this section are from the time when the Seidel family had recently moved to Barrytown, living in faculty housing on the campus of Unification Theological Seminary. Dietrich was teaching theology, and Elisabeth cared for their children as well as volunteering with various activities on campus.

Reverend and Mrs. Moon visited the campus a few times each year, and their children more often. During their visits, they were served meals in the VIP dining room. Serving them food was one of the activities Elisabeth enjoyed.

The food was prepared by several women who had been trained in Korean cooking by Mrs. Kim, wife of Seminary President David S.C. Kim. She spoke fluent Japanese but limited English and so those hired to cook under her tutelage were predominantly Japanese, usually wives of students or staff members.

As well as Elisabeth, a number of staff members and wives of faculty and staff members constituted the volunteer serving staff. Mentioned in these entries are Marie Ang, wife of Executive Vice President Dr. Edwin Ang, Traudl Byrne, wife of faculty member Dr. Shawn Byrne, and staff members Susan Cugini and Barbara Peat.

When the Moon children visited campus, they often spent time in the barn where a shooting range had been set up. On some occasions, refreshments were served to them in this barn. They would also spend time hunting on the 250-acre campus, which was home to wild turkeys, deer, and many other forms of wildlife.

This volume belongs to

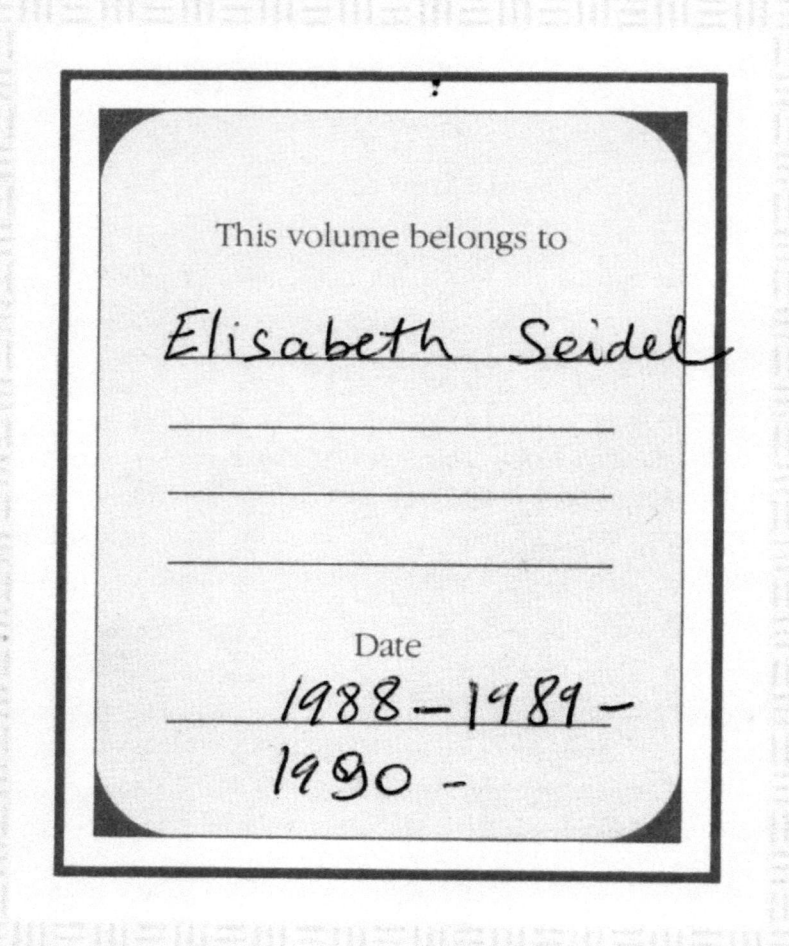

Elisabeth Seidel

Date
1988 — 1989 —
1990 —

Easter Sunday - April 3, 1988: Return to Belvedere

This morning we woke up early and went to Belvedere to hear Father. He talked about trees and the importance of their roots.

It changed from ten years ago! Brothers and sisters went through much suffering and sacrifice during that time. I felt they were all different: mature but burdened. In 1976 we were so exuberant when we saw Father and Mother. Somehow, I felt this time was gone and felt nostalgia about the earlier days.

As we were invited to go to East Garden for a celebration, we drove there after the talk. We knew two days earlier about the celebration and I had been thinking about how to have the right heart to go there.

The place is splendid. We entered the new house[20] built of marble and we had the feeling of entering a holy temple. This is the house of the Messiah. And here I am going to celebrate with him and True Mother. The banquet room looked like a king and queen's palace. David S.C. Kim was the MC, and he asked everyone to come in and stand by their chairs. Many Korean members were there. It seems that they are the core of the church. I was amazed to see so many Asian faces.

---

[20] The original house at the East Garden estate was relatively small and inadequate for holding large gatherings. The new house was constructed over a period of years, and once completed it became the location for Reverend Moon's sermons as well as banquets and other gatherings.

True Parents and True Family came, and Peter Kim[21] gave some introductory remarks. It was the Eight-day Ceremony of the first son of Hyun Jin nim (third son of True Parents) and Reverend Kwak's daughter, Jun Sook, and the 26th birthday of Colonel Pak's son, Jin Sung.

Korean food was served, beautifully prepared with fancy plates and cups. As soon as we sat down to start eating, David Kim called "Dietrich Seidel" out loud and asked him to approach True Parents with his wife. We did not expect that, and I felt like in a dream. We walked toward the head table where True Parents were eating, and we made two full bows. David Kim bowed with us and explained to True Parents that Dietrich finished his Ph.D. under Dr. Richardson. Everyone applauded. I had eye contact with Mother and smiled at her. We went back to our chairs, and President Kim continued to explain to True Parents (in Korean but was translated by our neighbor) that some Ph.D. students did not make it because they could not keep the spiritual standard or tradition. Those who did succeed were usually those who kept this standard during their studies.

There were some songs and dancing after the meal. The new baby's parents looked so friendly and reachable.

We came back to the Seminary, and I feel I want to keep the high spiritual atmosphere which surrounded me at East Garden.

---

[21] Reverend Moon's assistant and interpreter.

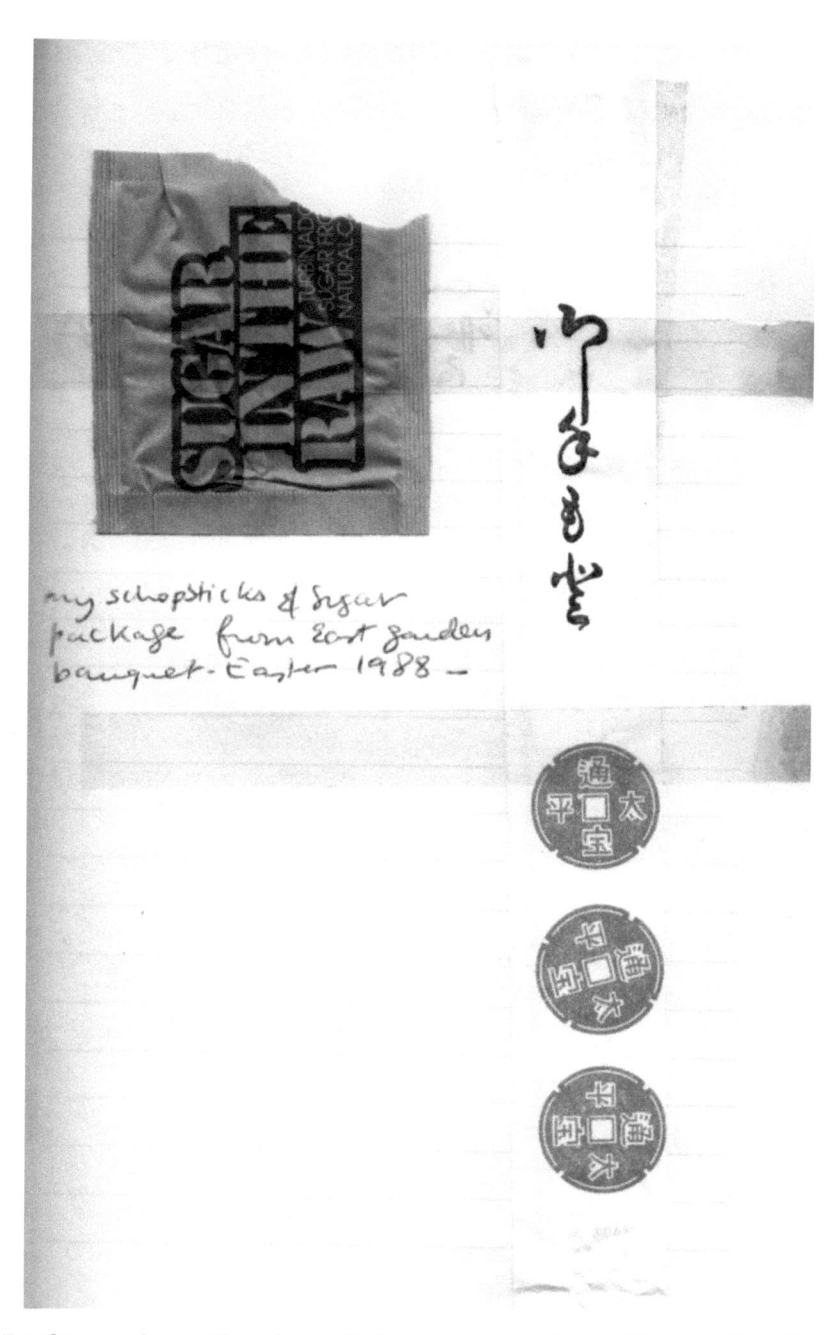

Packages from the chopsticks and sugar from the celebration meal, saved in Elisabeth's journal

June 29, 1988: Father Signed Dietrich's Thesis

True Parents came to Barrytown today. One day before graduation. They arrived shortly after 10:30 and went to their dining room. I have been helping Mrs. Ang to prepare snacks and drinks for True Parents, True Children and guests, and was supposed to help serve at lunch time.

When True Parents arrived, we made full bows (those who were going to serve) Mrs. Ang, Traudl Byrne, Susan Cugini and myself.

Then Mrs. Kim asked Susan Cugini and myself to bring flowers for True Parents to put on their blouse or shirt. I was nervous because I did not expect to do this and I did not know exactly how to do it, which side etc.? Then the pin seemed so hard to pierce through the flower that it bent. I was standing there feeling really terrible, holding the flower and hoping Mrs. Kim or Mrs. Ang would do it. But somehow Mrs. Kim pushed me to go to Father and do it. In my heart I said I do not know how I am going to make this flower hold on Father's shirt but I have to go to him and see what happens! I started touching True Father's shirt and said, "May I put this flower on your shirt Father?" Father said, "Put on the table!"

Then David Kim told Father I was Dietrich Seidel's wife and Father asked, "How old are you?" I answered, 43. The he asked through David Kim, do you have two or three children? I said, "two children, Father."

Mrs. Ang served coffee and McCol soda to True Parents. Father drank coffee and then two or three McCols. Mrs. Ang kept bringing new glasses of McCol. Father was wearing a blue and white striped shirt and Mother a black suit with a white handkerchief on the side.

All the graduates were sitting on the floor, and others tried to squeeze in through the kitchen door where Japanese sisters were busy cooking.

Father talked about true love. Also, he said in the past, you had to leave your hometown to go to other lands. Now I want to send you back to your hometown. This is the time to go back to the hometown and witness there.

After a while, True Mother left and went to her room. There she drank Ocean Spray pink grapefruit drink and one Japanese sister gave me the box and straw to keep as a souvenir.

To serve the lunch we had to be quick in setting the table. Susan and I were supposed to serve the guests.

After lunch, David Kim brought True Father the theses and Ph.D. diplomas of David Carlson and Dietrich Seidel for Father to sign. David Kim called me up again and said to represent my husband, who was away at a conference, to True Parents. So, I stood by True Parents as Father was signing. Then David Kim said I could go. After a while he called me back and said to thank True Parents for my husband, so I made two full bows to show my gratitude. Of course, I could not understand what David Kim was saying in Korean. I only understood the word Canada, as he was showing Father the first page of Dietrich's thesis.

Then True Parents left very quickly. I heard that Mother wanted to go shopping on the way, so they went in different cars. Father with Hyo Jin nim and Mother with Kook Jin nim. We all waved goodbye.

Father Moon signing Dietrich's Ph.D. diploma and thesis while Mother Moon looks on. David Kim is assisting and Elisabeth is standing behind him.

May 26, 1989: Coke, Favorite Drink of Hyun Jin nim

Today Hyun Jin nim, the third son of True Parents, came to Barrytown as he did many times in the past two months. I served Whoppers from Burger King. He asked for some cheese and said Coke is his favorite drink.

Marie France Kirkley had made French pastry and he seemed surprised and happy. He asked who made it. Mrs. Ang said her name and that she was my spiritual daughter. He said the French know how to make pastries. Then he said he had been learning French for a few years but it is a little too feminine a language for him.

Then he asked me if I spoke French. I told him I am French. He said, I thought you were Dukakis![22] He had told me before that I looked like Dukakis' assistant.

Then he said Mother once told him that the French colonized Korea. He said that the first missionaries were very grateful to the French nation. Then he went on speaking about the importance of learning Korean.

I served him coffee and then I had to go to a parents' meeting to organize summer activities for the children. Mrs. Ang stayed. He went on talking about how he likes people who are genuine. He said he bows to Father because he really loves Father not because of his position. We should bow to him because we love him too.

It felt so good to see him.

---

[22] Michael Dukakis, Governor of Massachusetts and Democratic presidential candidate in 1988.

May 31, 1989: Another Cake by Marie France

Today Hyun Jin nim came to Barrytown, around 5:00 pm. Sometimes it seems that there are a few obstacles to overcome when the True Children come. For example, getting ready, or start cooking, etc.

At 6 pm I called Doug, saying that the Japanese sisters are starting to cook, and it will be ready in about an hour. At 6:30 I called back saying dinner will be ready in about 10 minutes. They came at 7:40, and had some soup, rice, Korean meat, kimchee, melon with orange slices and another cake that Marie France Kirkley made yesterday.

Hyun Jin nim came in first and was waiting for Doug and one friend. I brought him soup and he asked me if I have a family. I said we have two children and my husband is teaching here. Then he asked how old are the children and if my husband had a PhD. I said nine and eleven, and my husband got his PhD in Toronto. He asked if he is very tall with glasses. I said, tall but no glasses. And he asked, what is his name.

He liked the soup, ate two bowls and asked if we made the cake just for them. He drank two or three cups of coffee.

Then he took two Cokes from the fridge to drink on the way and left. We went to the circle to wave goodbye.

September 1, 1989: $100 Bill

Hyun Jin nim and Kwon Jin nim came to Barrytown today, together with Chaim Durst. They ate dinner in the VIP dining room at 8:30, together with Doug Williams (Security) and David Ang and Goon Koch.

Eiko Suzuki and Eiko Endo cooked, and Barbara Peat and myself served. Kwon Jin nim asked for some milk. They (the True Children) asked each one sitting at the table to sing. Doug sang "Praise God, Praise God."

When they left, Hyun Jin nim handed me a $100 bill and said this is for the kitchen staff: "The meal was delicious. You should go out together." They left to go and see the movie "Relentless." We went out to the circle and waved goodbye to all of them.

December 23, 1989: More to Eat

Five True Children (Hyun Jin nim, Kook Jin nim, Kwon Jin nim, Young Jin nim, and Hyung Jin nim) came to visit the Seminary today. First they went to the barn, then outside for target practice. It was bitter cold.

Then they came to the VIP dining room to eat. Eiko Endo and another Japanese sister prepared the meal for them. Mrs. Ang and I set the table and served them. Diesa and Jenny Ang were in the kitchen for a few minutes when they first arrived.

Before the meal Kook Jin nim prayed. Mrs. Ang heard the prayer and she told me he prayed that they will never forget to be sacrificial and then for the beautiful surroundings here in Barrytown, the creation they can experience.

They seemed to enjoy the meal very much. Hyun Jin nim is drinking a lot of coffee. He once said that Coke is his favorite drink, so we had Coke for each of them. At the end they also had hot chocolate with marshmallows.

I brought the Christmas candies (*papillottes*) sent to me from France. The younger children said, "Oh, candies!" first when they came, but nobody seems to have eaten any.

Then they left and asked to take hot chocolate to go. We went to the circle to wave goodbye to them.

March 22, 1990: We All Have to Grow

The True Children came frequently these last few days. We served lunch and dinner and brought it to the barn. We always have to be on our toes to make sure we are ready when Hyo Jin nim is ready.

Madeleine and Julie are usually hanging around by the barn when they come. Actually, they have been hunting with them since Mr. Suzuki went to Korea. Madeleine said Hyo Jin nim spoke to them for quite a while. He was asking a lot of questions: Who are your professors, how do the students feel about the True Children, how is their relationship with the True Children, do they miss me when I do not speak in Belvedere? He also said he would have become very cocky (arrogant) but he realized in his position the most important quality was to be humble.

Later on Mrs. Ang shared with us about Hyo Jin nim's tumultuous teenage years. He used to go fast on his motorcycle and said everything belongs to me, etc. It seems everyone, including the True Children, have to go through the growth stage.

Jin Hun nim, the husband of True Parents' third daughter Un Jin nim, is studying here at the Seminary. He is a junior student and we have to find out the right relationship with him, how to attend him and support him.

Letter to Friends, December 7, 1989

Dear Friends,

Greetings from the Unification Theological Seminary (UTS) in Barrytown, New York. We hope everything is going well with you and that this letter will find you in good health and good spirits.

As you may know, I [Dietrich] have been teaching theology at UTS since I graduated from the University of St. Michael's College in June, 1987. I have been teaching courses in Theology such as: Fall and Redemption, Christian Denominations, Eschatology, Marriage and Family in the Christian Tradition, etc.

I continue to cherish fond memories of my studies at the Toronto School of Theology, and will always be grateful for the openness of heart and the high standards of all my professors who taught me there.

Here at UTS I like the challenge to always be in the avant-garde for ecumenism and to participate in conferences which are being held here. A few weeks ago, scholars from four continents came here to speak about "The Love of God in the World's Religions." Indeed, it was an inspiring and meaningful meeting as we shared as brothers and sisters under one Heavenly Father.

In June, 1990, I am planning to attend another Schleiermacher research seminar with scholars from Europe and North America. Our group of scholars has been bound together through several exciting conferences, especially during our trip to East Germany a year ago.

Through our children we always feel a strong connection with Canada, where they were born during the struggles of graduate studies!

The Seidel family at UTS

Christopher and Diesa are growing fast; they are now 11 and 9. Christopher loves books and airplanes. He discussed being a test pilot. He is very serious about his studies. Diesa prefers sports, music and art. After school they enjoy activities with their friends such as martial arts, riding their bikes, riding horses, cleaning the barn, going for walks on trails (you can walk in the forest for hours); the UTS property consists of 250 acres of land, including a man-made pond.

If you happen to travel in this area, we would like to invite you to visit our Seminary amid the beautiful surrounding countryside. UTS is situated in the Mid-Hudson Valley, about a 20-minute drive from the city of Kingston. It is a place where students from every part of the world come to study theology and related subjects. The professors here are from different religious traditions like Judaism, Greek Orthodox, Catholicism, Protestantism and Unificationism.

You are welcome to bring your family and stay for a few days. I am sure you will like it here. Let us know when you plan to come, so that we can reserve a guest room (or rooms) for you.

We wish you and your loved ones a Merry Christmas and a Happy New Year. May God bless you abundantly in the New Year.

Dietrich and Elisabeth Seidel

Letter to Friends, December 17, 1991

Dear Friends,

We hope this letter finds you and your loved ones in good health and in joyful expectation of this Christmas season.

The year of 1991 comes to a close soon and we feel inspired to share with you some of its highlights from our life here at the Unification Theological Seminary (UTS).

As can be expected, this has been an eventful year at UTS. Many times we welcomed various groups of visitors at the seminary. We met Islamic leaders from Egypt and Jordan, community leaders from Korea and students and professors from the Soviet Union. All of these visitors were supportive of the Unification Movement.

Besides my regular teaching activities (teaching Theology courses in the Master of Divinity and Religious Education programs) we also conducted a number of seminars. Some of them dealt with health and spirituality; others with family ethics or campus ministry.

My wife enjoys organizing these seminars and wants to help whenever there is a need to bring people together, such as community events or interfaith work. She is also my indispensable assistant in my work as class advisor and student counselor.

Presently, I am preparing to teach a course on Marriage and Family from a theological perspective. It will also include contemporary moral issues. Beyond this course we are challenged to practice our reflections at home by going through a phase of parental testing with two adolescent children who will soon reach the ages of 12 and 14.

Christopher is ambitious and likes to win. Because of this determination he was lucky to carry home some trophies from school competitions. Diesa recently broke her right arm and is looking forward to having the cast removed at the beginning of January. She is always cheerful, loving sports and social life.

Looking back at the events of this past year we are always amazed at how Reverend Moon is continuously initiating new activities to promote world peace and unify the world's religions. In particular, his meeting with President Gorbachev and his recent meeting with North Korea's leader, Kim Il Sung, point to a hopeful future for the re-unification of Korea and the final elimination of the threat of communism.

Also of interest, a few months ago a book about Reverend Moon's trial in America was published. *"Inquisition: The Persecution and Prosecution of the Reverend Sun Myung Moon,"* by a Pulitzer Prize winning journalist, covers much of the movement's history in America. As you can imagine, we are quite excited about this and hope that soon public opinion about the Unification Movement will change for the better.

If your busy schedule allows, we will always be happy to welcome you here on campus. Just give us a call so we can reserve a room for you.

May you experience the joys of a Merry Christmas and may God bless you throughout the New Year.

With heartfelt greetings,

Dietrich and Elisabeth Seidel

Prayer to Conclude 1997

Dear Heavenly Father,

Thank you for Your love!

I am so, so sorry that You cried so much in 1997. But True Parents could dry up some of Your tears on November 29th.[23]

How much we have to take care of You by taking care of the world. I am so, so sorry that I did not do enough this year of 1997. Especially not loving people enough with true love. Not forgiving enough. Not living up to Your standard. Not bringing people to the RFK Stadium. Not Blessing enough people. Not praying enough, and not reading enough Divine Principle and other speeches.

I want to do so much for You and I must cry upon my limitations and shortcomings. I want to really love You with true love by loving True Parents, my spouse, my children, my brothers and sisters. And I see how much blocked I am to become a true spouse, true sister, true mother. The force of true love must govern the universe and must govern me.

The waves of the ocean announce Your presence and Your power and Your eternity, and wash away all sins and dirt from the earth.

---

[23] The World Culture and Sports Festival, held in Washington DC, included a Holy Marriage Blessing ceremony held at RFK Stadium on November 29, 1997.

Reconciliation and Mending of Relationships between France and Austria-Germany in My Own Family

The French suffered greatly from the Germans and Austrians throughout the Second World War. Considering such past injuries, would they be able to accept a marriage between a French person and one of Austrian-German nationality? The answer in my case was negative; this was not a step they were willing to take easily.

Let me describe briefly my in-laws' position, which I discovered when we traveled to Europe after my children were born, and Dietrich was completing the last leg toward his Ph.D. degree.

Soon after the euphoria of our wedding, I realized that my husband's family was not really thrilled about having a Moonie and foreigner as a daughter-in-law. Dietrich's mom, Margaretha, first married during World War II. Her husband, Friedmar Seidel, was an officer who worked quite close to Hitler. I saw a picture of him with Hitler. His life during the war was mostly kept a secret, although a few facts remained.

Margaretha gave birth to her two children, Gisela and Dietrich, in a special home for mothers destined to start a new race. In fact, the selection had started at her marriage, since her particular features were required (blue eyes, plus a certain height and weight) in order to marry a service man. She did not know the whereabouts of her husband, only that he was undergoing tough training, so harsh and inhuman in fact that it drove several of his comrades to suicide. After the war, Friedmar and Margaretha divorced. Later she remarried, to Dr. Cyril Vesely, who became Dietrich's step-father.

Dietrich's parents, Margaretha and Friedmar Seidel

A few years after my children were born, we visited my parents and my large tribe of 400+ family (and still counting!) in France. I was truly excited to introduce them to my new Austrian relatives with their pictures. However, when my mother saw Friedmar in full uniform that included the Nazi insignia, she fell into a panic, exclaiming "Please hide this picture and never ever show it to anyone around here!"

Indeed, my family and tribe had suffered a lot from the war, and notably a young cousin had lost her speech through trauma, only recovering later in her childhood. She wanted to show Dietrich around her town, where Germans and Austrians had committed crimes. One household had a mother and her child killed, another a young soldier killed in combat, and some so traumatized that they did not even want to hear the sound of the German language. All the while, my young kids were running around the table shouting, "My dad is a Nazi baby!"

At that point, it became abundantly clear that our marriage (Matching and Blessing initiated by Father Sun Myung Moon of Korea) had a specific purpose – to mend the relationships between two countries and two families.

Our parents fought wars with physical weapons. We were meant to fight a spiritual battle and bring a victorious reconciliation through love. Although we were settled in North America, we endeavored to visit Europe (Austria and France) every two to three years. At the beginning, we had family reunions with my many relatives in France. We would conduct Holy Wine Ceremonies, while talking about the ideals of peace and the value of these special gatherings. My mother wondered about my zeal and frenzy over my unusual involvement with my family and tribe. She would advise me not to pray before the public meals, although in private she had become accustomed to her theologian son-in-law, who would often recite some prayers in French.

When Dietrich was in the later stages of his Ph.D. thesis, we decided to spend a few months in Europe, as he did not need to be in residence at his university in Canada. Money was tight, and we thought that it would be economical to live with our respective families, since they had welcomed us before. Then we began to experience great waves of spiritual reaction to our sojourn there. Restoration, or the need for it, was felt at its peak, and drama became our way of life. In Austria, I felt rejected by my in-laws, due to my beliefs, my Moonie status and my foreign status. As an additional hindrance, Dietrich's thesis was overdue, progress at every level was slow, and we ran out of funds. We were beginning to depend on Dietrich's family, and they in turn wanted to control our lives.

Suddenly, I was put on a train to France along with our two children, a symbolic re-enactment of World War II in my own family. I had the distinct feeling that my in-laws were trying to separate us and perhaps find a better match for my husband – a person from their own country, naturally!

Our difficulties to communicate around that time seemed to prove this. When I was trying to reach my husband in Austria from my hometown in St. Jean, I was not able to do so on most days. I was told that he was not there or busy studying. Our letters reflected all the tensions we were experiencing. Would my husband's faith survive this ordeal? Would he return to his own family? Would he stand for God and finish his thesis, resisting his relatives' influence and control?

I begged God to let us return quickly to the USA – land of the brave, land of the free! Curiously, the minute we set foot in America, miraculously every conflict or spiritual war seemed to vanish into thin air. We breathed freely, indeed. As I never forgot that our marriage was made for the sake of our nations, I could hang on.

We continued to visit our families every two to three years since that tumultuous time. We organized family reunions, even extending them to the level of Ambassadors for Peace.

One year, arriving in France across the English Channel, we landed in Brittany and rented a car to reach my hometown in the Alps. We got lost while driving, and ended up at Omaha Beach; and this happened not just once, but again and again! We kept going around in circles, always arriving back on Omaha Beach. We realized that it was a sign that we ought to stop and pray there, especially at the cemetery where so many American soldiers were buried. The spirit to pray for reconciliation pushed us on to visit many other war memorials in the surrounding regions of my hometown. We made a condition for the first three days to call each soldier by his name, and we also invited friends and contacts to participate with us in the reconciliation events. I also asked my great uncle Maxime to work with me and be in charge of such programs, albeit "on the other side."

With the beginning of the Hometown Providence, in 2003 we decided that we ought to remain in Europe for longer periods of time. Dietrich could teach courses at Webster University and at the International University of Vienna. We picked a local restaurant to hold our monthly meetings, as the owner was a long-time student of my husband's courses and had treated us with a dinner on many occasions.[24] The scope of the dinners expanded as we included professors, students and others we had met. We honored several professors with an Ambassador for Peace award. One university president and his wife became very close to us. Once, they spent a whole day with us, eating, walking, sharing, and watching videos that included Father Moon as the founder of the Family Federation for World Peace. Then,

---

[24] Spetim Redo, owner of the Shooters restaurant. A brief account of these meetings is included in the entries on "Ecumenical Work" in the final section of this book.

we would attend their Jewish community service along with them. A large interfaith forum was set up at the university on the basis of Dietrich's class on World Religions.

Reconciliation Event in St. Jean de Maurienne

During the summer, we would go to my hometown in the French Alps and hold reconciliation events there every September 2nd, as it was the anniversary of the liberation of St. Jean de Maurienne, commemorating the date when the last German-Austrian soldier left the area. On that date, the city hosts a huge pageant with music and pomp, and deploys a delegation of veterans to speak at the war memorial. Once, as we greeted the Mayor there, he pointed out that the worst crimes were committed by Austrians. Dietrich felt that it was appropriate to compose a letter to be read at our event – a letter in which he would repent for the heinous crimes that had taken place in his wife's hometown and ask for forgiveness. This letter was later sent to many officials in the town.[25]

During the first such event, we gave 12 Ambassadors for Peace awards. Among the recipients was one 90-year-old lady, who received it because of her relatives' courage in hiding a Jewish family in their own home. One professor of German language acknowledged that she had been waiting for such an event for a long time. Her grandfather had been saved because a German soldier gave him his uniform to allow him to escape. He had asked his granddaughter to promise him to work for the reconciliation of the two nations: France and Germany. Other beautiful stories of heroism came out: One man testified that, as a child, he had befriended the dog of a German officer; and during a bomb raid, that officer covered him with his own body to protect him from harm. Through sharing these stories, people became close in heart and everyone felt that they belonged to a great family, desiring to make a new and better human world.

In the following years, we had a delegation of Austrians who performed songs and musical pieces. We held one event in a restaurant and another in the Catholic Church in La Chambre, which is my original hometown. After asking permission of the priest there, he told us later that he could not sleep over this decision. He admitted that it had been a real challenge to support our project; and some people on the Veterans Association Board did not want to grant us permission. I wrote a letter to the mayor of the town, mentioning to him that my great uncle died for his country, that my grandfather had served this community as the

---

[25] A copy of this letter, translated into English, is included in the entries on "Persecution and Reconciliation" in the final section of this book.

Assistant Mayor and that we wished to recognize them as well. So finally, permission was granted; and two years in a row, we prayed and offered flowers at the War Memorial with a French-German delegation, totaling 70 guests for both events.

The war had caused much pain to the French people of my hometown, but they welcomed such reconciliation events between the victims and their victimizers. We considered it a great victory to have survived what felt like "World War III" between our families and kept our faith in Reverend and Mrs. Moon's vision of a world of peace and unity under one loving God.

The River of Life Goes On

The world had entered the new millennium, with much hope for this new beginning both in the secular world and the religious world, including the Unification Movement. It was expected and hoped that the suffering and sacrifice of the early members would lead to a plentiful harvest. However, that was a simplistic and idealistic expectation. In reality, the work of establishing God's Kingdom on earth takes not a few years but many generations.

This time in Elisabeth's life is another transition, a time when many of her loved ones, including her parents and her beloved husband, passed into the spiritual world. For the Unification Movement, it was not just the older members who made this transition, but Reverend Moon himself, at the beginning of September 2012.

After her husband, Dietrich, passed in 2016, Elisabeth found recordings of a course he had taught on "Life after Life." We worked together to publish a book, entitled *Eternal Life in the Spirit World*, based on these classes together with my own research.

Naturally, with the passing of so many dear to her, Elisabeth developed a great interest in the afterlife. She began to read books, meet with mediums, and watch shows about people's near-death experiences, angels, and those who channel spirits who have departed the earth. Many of the entries in this section deal with the phenomenon of dying and the transition to the spirit world.

While some of the entries deal with struggle and pain and loss, there are many others that are filled with humor and love. Several describe the connection that holds strong between those on earth and their beloveds who have made the transition. It is truly love that transcends the barrier between the physical and spiritual realms, love that is the most powerful force in the cosmos. It provides the energy for the river of our lives to flow on eternally.

For ease of reading, this section is subdivided into a number of different topics: Family, Persecution and Reconciliation, Ecumenical Work, Restoration of Beloved France, Living with God, Help from Heaven; and the final topic, the conclusion of her search for true love: Dietrich, Eternal Loving Spouse.

Family

Here we learn more about Elisabeth's family, both their past and more recent times.

The first entry, an interview Elisabeth conducted with Dietrich's mother in 2006, is very significant. As she talks about her life during the war, we realize that the Austrians and Germans suffered too. It becomes clear that in wartime both those on the side of the aggressors and their victims suffer. Everyone suffers, even the perpetrators of the atrocities. With this realization, forgiveness becomes possible, leading to reconciliation, something that features strongly in Elisabeth's life.

Then there are two entries about her father, from whom she inherited several strong character traits.

These are followed by an entry about her daughter, Diesa, when she was young, and then a letter she sent to her family one Christmas, and the reply her son, Christopher, sent her.

Finally, there are two entries about her mother-in-law, Oma, one of which also includes Dietrich's sister, Gisela. These are written in a more light-hearted and humorous style, and give much hope for the future, in sharp contrast to the first entry about their earlier life.

Interview with Dietrich's Mother, 2006

Dietrich's mother, Margaretha, from Vienna, Austria, was 16 the first time she met Friedmar Seidel, a German citizen. He had four years training under Hitler, a very difficult training. Of those who began this difficult training, half of them collapsed, many committing suicide. She never asked about those times.

Dietrich's mother, Margaretha Stechauer, age 17

Then Friedmar went back to Germany for two years. His parents lived near Altenburg, in the part which became East Germany.

Margaretha went to visit him when she was 18. She stayed for two days. On the way back to the train, Friedmar told her that he had a relationship with a movie star.

Friedmar Seidel at home with his parents

She went back to Vienna and did not want to hear from him anymore. The next day, Friedmar came to Vienna to see her.

They married in 1942. She was 21 and Friedmar was 27. Friedmar was her first great love.

As the war was raging, she gave birth to two children, first Gisela in 1942 and then Dietrich in 1943, in the special home for mothers in Feichtenbach, in the small town of Pernitz, about 40 miles south of Vienna. This place became famous for producing babies from specially selected parents, with the plan to create a new beginning for humankind, a new "human race."

Home for mothers in Feichtenbach, Pernitz, where Dietrich and his sister, Gisela, were born

Friedmar was one of the security guards for Hitler, sometimes his driver. He had a tattoo on his arm, with "AH" written on it, as a security guard. After the war he could have been shot, so they burned it to hide the tattoo.

For one year and a quarter Margaretha did not see him, as he was in Germany. In 1945 she went to Germany with her young kids, Gisela and Dietrich, to visit. On the way, as they were crossing the fields, planes flew very low, attacking. They had to lie on the ground and play dead. There were many soldiers around, as the Russians had occupied Vienna.

When they were walking, Dietrich shouted "Please do not shoot."

They went to a cave as Margaretha was in shock and tired and did not know what to do. Then they walked to a farm. She felt guided and protected. Someone tapped her on the shoulder. It was Dr. Vesely, who later became her second husband.

Leopoldine and Michael Stechauer, Margaretha's parents and Dietrich's grandparents, in 1920

Another story from the wartime was that mothers and children could go to a farm in Tyrol. Margaretha had 10 minutes to pack up some food and get to the Danube to take a boat to Linz. On the boat there was only milk for the children. There was no food for four days. They stayed in Elmau in Tyrol from April until October, 1945.

Franz Muller, Leopoldine's father and Dietrich's great-grandfather, in 1925

After that they went back to Vienna. Their apartment had been taken over by the Russians who were occupying Austria. Margaretha had to go to the police to allow her to take back one room in the apartment.

Five young men where there, hiding in the apartment. It was in the 3rd district of Vienna, close to the Stadt Park. At the entrance of the building there were horses belonging to the Russians.

When Margaretha first lived in this apartment, in 1940, it was a residence for nobility; counts and countesses were living in the building.

Margaretha's mother, Leopoldine, had stayed behind in Vienna and could not find food. To save her energy she stayed in bed and ate one spoon of sugar in the morning and one spoon of sugar in the afternoon to survive. When Margaretha came back from the farm she was horrified to see how her mother looked – so skinny, like a ghost.

Perhaps these wartime experiences are the reason why my husband always wanted a large quantity of food to be served.

My Dad

He was blunt. He loved music and football. And he had a hot temper. Not everyone could take that.

I think I inherited those points from my father. With a calm appearance I have guts, hot temper, courage and conviction.

My Dad followed his guts. He did not care about the media and the fake news, or when everyone was saying "heresy, heresy, brainwashing, Moonies," and pointing fingers in ignorance and disbelief.

We said, "Pépé, Pépé, drink the Holy Wine. It is so good for you. He drank it, and quietly he signed the associate membership for the Holy Spirit Association for the Unification of World Christianity (HSA-UWC).

Henri Jamen, Elisabeth's father, holding the trophy won by the French National Basketball team when Diesa was its youngest member

He always trusted me and my husband. I believe the fact that he supported my family in this way gave him a better place in the spiritual world. Like the thief who said that Jesus had done nothing wrong when they were dying on the cross.

Jesus said to him, "Truly I tell you, today you will be with me in paradise" (Luke 23:43).

My Dad did not listen to the accusations. He followed his own path, like that thief who said kind words about Jesus. If even a thief can enter paradise, I believe my Dad can be blessed in heaven.

Also, Jesus said, "Then I will tell them plainly, 'I never knew you. Away from me, you evildoers!'" (Matthew 7:23) and "Jerusalem, Jerusalem, you who kill the prophets and stone those sent to you, how often I have longed to gather your children together, as a hen gathers her chicks under her wings, and you were not willing" (Matthew 23:37). Because the Pharisees were saying, "It is only by Beelzebub, the prince of demons, that this fellow drives out demons" (Matthew 12:24).

I wish so very much I could change the opinion in my country, France, where the people persecuted Reverend Moon because of the negative articles in the media, and treated us members so badly. If I had one wish, I would like to rectify this mistake.

On Dying Alone

I regret that my dad had to die alone. Nobody should.

I was in the US, planning to be in France in May and struggling with my own health situation. My brother, who lived close by, did what he could.

The doctor at the retirement home where he was living, I believe, gave him an overdose of medication to calm him down, because he was agitated at first and irritated as his needs were not being met. Food and drink did not arrive as he wished.

Instead of someone taking the time to talk to him, he was medicated for the peace of everyone, the staff and the patients. For weeks he was in this state of heavy medication, not able to feed himself. Several times I asked the nurse to put the phone to his ear and heart and I could talk to him and reassure him.

I am looking forward to see a loving community where people love and assist each other in time of need. Yes, we can.

My dad died alone.

In the afterlife, the sun and moon are shining, and everyone will have the possibility to love and be loved, even if they could not do it on earth.

Orphans and Orphanages

When I was visiting San Diego where my children live, we were finishing dinner together and my beloved son Christopher took out his wallet to pay for the family. As I looked at his wallet made of cloth, it was so falling apart, broken, and dirty, I was wondering why he does not buy a new one. He said this wallet had so much value and meaning because it comes from an orphanage where he bought it and he wants to send it somewhere for repair because it is so special to him.

There are so many causes to care for, why an orphanage? Then it hit me, orphanage: the kids without parents. How can a child be without a mom and dad and not receiving the love he or she is longing for? When I was a child, I always asked my Grandma Marie to tell me stories about her life in an orphanage in Lyon in France, where I guess her mom must have dropped her off for reasons we do not know.

When my Grandma was still a child, perhaps seven or eight years old, in the summer she would go to a family in the mountains of Savoie in "Les Côtes" by Saint Etienne de Cuines. In exchange for helping to take care of the fields and animals, she would receive room and board. After the summer it was time for her to go back by train, and I believe one lady from the orphanage would come and wait for her at the train station in Saint Avre-La Chambre. Marie refused to board the train, clinging to this couple who took care of her during the summer, holding their coats and sobbing. No-one could persuade her to get on the train. This couple, already with many kids, decided to adopt her and they became her new family.

Her new brothers and sisters became close with her, and when I was a child I met many of them and later their offspring. I heard they even gave her a dowry when she married my grandfather Jean Jamen, himself without a father. His mom had two children and the older one took care of Jean when his mom passed and was his only parent or witness for his wedding. They said that his father must have been an Italian man coming to France for work and had a love affair there in Monthion, a village close to Italy.

Even though my Grandma Marie was an adopted child coming from an orphanage, her adoptive parents considered her as their most beloved child, and she could be raised in a loving family with brothers and sisters.

The love of parents is one of the most precious of all. Parents do not keep grudges against their children, or bad feelings. They do not keep any record of wrong. Their love is infinite and eternal. It was a great blessing for my Grandma Marie to be adopted by loving parents.

I am Your Child, Please Always Check on Me

When my daughter was young and we could not be at home at her bed time, she used to leave loving notes for us, her parents. "Dear Mommy and Daddy, I love you a lot! Please check on me right now." "Mom, all I need from you is love."

For Father's Day, she said "Out of everything I learned from you, the things that I will always remember are the things that nourish the heart. You are an inspiration to me because of your unconditional love that you give, unconditionally." "Dad, I still remember the very first thing you ever taught me … What it feels like to be loved."

To be a parent, we learn to love unconditionally. This is why all of us should become a parent, to grow and feel God's heart, because He loves us as a parent. Parental heart makes us more complete, more whole. Then we can love others too, as a parent.

If for any reason we cannot have children, then we can adopt, or be a foster parent, or adopt a loving animal with whom we can share our abundant love.

I am Always Grateful

Christmas, 2002

I am grateful for God, my angels, my ancestors and for all the saints, past and present, who provide me with spiritual guidance. I am grateful for Jesus, Muhammad, Buddha, Confucius and all the spiritual masters. I am grateful for the revelation God is giving in our time.

I am grateful for my life, my family, my eternal husband, my beloved son and daughter, my parents, my in-laws, my church friends and my very special circle sisters.

I am grateful for all prayers for world peace and reconciliation.

I am grateful for my faith in the new world to come.

On Gratitude

> From my son, Christopher after receiving the previous letter, entitled "I am Always Grateful"

Dear Mom and Dad and Diesa,

Merry Christmas! Thank you for your note on gratitude, Mom. It's always a good idea to count our blessings in life – something we frequently forget.

I will miss seeing you all this Christmas time, but I also know that on a deeper level we are all connected in spirit. It is this spiritual connection that always keeps us together even if we cannot see each other in physical form.

Please say hello to all friends and family during this Christmas, and also send my greetings to all the relatives, that all is going well in Brazil.

I plan to be working at a bread shop for Christmas time with a friend, baking bread and pastries as a small Christmas business venture. The island is very beautiful – all the roads in the town are just made of sand – so there are no cars and just horses. The beaches are beautiful and I have already walked for miles and miles with nobody in sight and just more beaches. The sunsets are also very beautiful and it feels relaxed, a little like Aruba.

Much love and blessings and hugs,

Chris

Elisabeth with Dietrich, his mother, Margaretha (Oma), and sister, Gisela, at the famous Prater in Vienna

The Escapades of Oma and Gisela

This summer Oma,[26] my 97 years old mother-in-law, and her daughter Gisela, suffering from Alzheimer's disease, both entered a retirement home in the center of Vienna, Austria. They quickly adapted pretty well.

Oma's room is spacious and beautiful with four large windows that let the outside light in, large sofas for the whole family to gather, and many pictures of loved ones.

---

[26] After her marriage to Dietrich, Elisabeth called his mother "Oma," which means Grandma in German.

Gisela's room is next to Oma's, each having their private bathroom. There is a small kitchen in the middle. I did not know someone can have a suite in this kind of place!

There is a garden downstairs. In the summer they sit under the tree, sipping Viennese coffee with *Sachertorte* (chocolate cake), Oma's favorite!

Every day Oma puts on a beautiful dress and always a necklace which goes with the dress. She combs her hair with style, as only she can do, having been a hairdresser as her profession. They live in style!

They both could not function any more on their own in their private apartment. So the seniors home seemed a good fit for them, as unfortunately no one was able to take care of them in their own home.

After a time, they started to get a little bored and wanted to take a walk or go somewhere.

The first time they went out while the door guardian was not looking, Oma tried her best to be able to walk properly, holding tight to Gisela's arm. Soon enough they reached Mariahilfer Strasse, a famous street in the center of Vienna. And soon enough they were lost, not remembering how to come back. Gisela decided to go and find out by herself the way back, and asked Oma to wait by a corner of the street in order not to get exhausted by walking too much.

Gisela found her way and arrived back at the retirement home. In the mean time she forgot about Oma. There she met Sami her grandson, and great-grandson of Oma, who had been called by the staff when they realized that the two ladies were missing. Sami asked Gisela, where is Oma? Gisela answered that she did not know. So Sami started praying how to find Oma. After going up and down the neighborhood, he decided to inform the police, as Oma was nowhere to be seen. When he entered the police station, Oma was sitting there. Someone had just brought her there. So they happily went back to the retirement home.

A second time the two ladies could escape, Sami was called again. Sami is 27, a born-again preacher or on the way to becoming one. I like Sami a lot because his heart is very big and he tries to be like Jesus. He loves to preach and he always prays. He never misses an opportunity to preach, like this morning when we went for some errands together. We picked up Trudi, the other 97 years old cousin of Oma, who wanted to visit her relatives. He truly wanted to convince me that we are saved by grace. Sami is always praying, which I respect a lot. So, Sami was called to find the two ladies again.

Sami prayed again, where could the two grandmas be? The thought came to him: Maybe Mariahilfer Strasse, or Gisela's place, or Oma's place.

When he finally arrived at Oma's home, there they were standing by the door, as they had no keys to enter. A charitable neighbor was waiting with them.

Sami asked the two ladies, how did they get here? Neither of them could remember. But here they were.

So Sami, while praying, thought of a plan. He put all the family members on Instagram. There are quite a few members, including the grand kids. And everyday someone from the family goes to the retirement home and takes Oma and Gisela for an excursion, or something special.

They go for coffee in a special restaurant or ice cream and cake, or around the corner there is a big aquarium with many floors. Oma sits in her wheelchair, and has been brought already to many different floors there. They really enjoy seeing all the different multicolored fishes. There was a monkey as well who happened to jump on Oma's lap. It was fun. Sometimes when the weather is very bad, they have afternoon games.

Elisabeth with Sami visiting Oma and Gisela

Each and every one is willing to help Grandma and Great-grandma to have a more happy and meaningful time in their golden age, to feel loved and cared for.

Without the true love compassion and care of the family their lives would be meaningless, sad and lonely without a purpose. I am so grateful to praying Samuel that he found a way to show love and care for his loved ones. We love you Sami, we love you Oma and Gisela.

In the meantime, Oma and Gisela each got a bracelet with the address of their living quarters.

The Great Love

As I was visiting my 97 years young mother-in-law in Vienna, I was surprised that she was still reading books. I thought she was only looking through magazines, or mainly watching tv as entertainment, or playing dominos, if she was not on an excursion.

Elisabeth with her mother-in-law

But to my surprise she was reading a book from the American author Pearl Buck, and the title was "Die Große Liebe," means "Le Grand Amour" or "The Great Love."

Wow! She is 97 and reading love stories! I realized this ideal of ours never dies. At 100 you can still dream about love, true love, the one and only. This quest never ever ends, and reading about it becomes so exciting, interesting and fulfilling.

I told Oma, I know who is my great love for ever and ever. And she had me tell her again and again my encounter with Dietrich, her son, which was love at first sight. And how it stayed this way during our 40 years of married life and beyond.

Persecution and Reconciliation

This section continues the dual themes of persecution and reconciliation, both of which have featured significantly in Elisabeth's stories.

The first entry is an account of Elisabeth's visit to Israel, a pilgrimage to many of the holy sites of the Abrahamic faiths. As is Elisabeth's nature, she involved herself in bringing together representatives of enemy nations.

Next, is a copy of the letter of repentance Dietrich wrote as part of the reconciliation event they organized on the anniversary of the liberation of St. Jean de Maurienne from the Austrian-German armies.

The subsequent entries relate to persecution Elisabeth has suffered as a follower of Reverend Sun Myung Moon, particularly in her hometown. Although deeply hurt by the way her former friends, neighbors, and city officials turned against her, she recognized that they were being influenced by the barrage of negativity from the media. She found it in her heart to forgive them, as Jesus asked God to forgive those who condemned him, saying: "Father forgive them, for they know not what they do" (Luke 23:34).

The final entry is a heartwarming letter sent to Elisabeth by her daughter, Diesa, comforting and encouraging her after one of the painful encounters, and ending this topic with a reminder "to always have sunshine in your heart."

Visit to the Holy Land

The people of the Holy Land touched my heart so deeply. In the Sea of Galilee, I felt so many spirit beings from 2000 years ago in the time of Jesus, traveling with us in the replica of Jesus' boat. It was one of the most meaningful trips of my life.

I picked up some stones on the hill where the Sermon on the Mount was given. The breathtaking beauty of this place must have inspired Jesus so much. It is as beautiful as every word that Jesus spoke there.

We went to Bethlehem where Jesus was born. There we saw the Shepherds' Field. I bought a necklace from a passionate Palestinian young man who was struggling to feed his family. At first, I said no thank you to so many peddlers, group after group trying to sell us something. But this particular person was so desperate that his children could not eat if he was not going to sell this necklace. Ask and it shall be given, I felt.

I also became close friends with a Jewish lady and a Palestinian lady. Both passionate and God-loving, true to their beliefs, so sincere. Many times, I felt like a mother reconciling her fighting children. Was it not the first tragedy of Cain killing Abel in the first family? My Palestinian friend just lost her husband on the street, killed by a Jew, she said.

At the Holocaust museum I walked through the museum with a French lady married with a Jew. She was sobbing all the way. Representing Austria, I repented for all the killings of the Jews by my in-laws from Germany and Austria, and asked God, may Your Kingdom come now.

Letter of Repentance

Written by Dietrich Seidel to ask forgiveness for the crimes perpetrated by Austrians and Germans on the occasion of the ceremony commemorating the anniversary of the liberation of St. Jean de Maurienne

September 2, 2009

Monsieur le Préfet de la Savoie
Monsieur le Maire de St. Jean de Maurienne

It is with a sincere heart that today I offer my deepest apologies for the war crimes. I have a German father, an Austrian mother and a French wife, and our countries were torn apart by the two World Wars. Each year we remember and honor the many French citizens who sacrificed their lives for France.

My wife is Elisabeth Jamen Seidel, who was born in Chambery, grew up in La Chambre and St. Jean, and whose ancestors suffered so much during the German occupation. Among others, her great uncle Maxime Bartholomé is buried in Verdun among so many other French young men.

Today I ask for the grace of a new beginning of reconciliation and of eternal peace not only between my wife's ancestors and my ancestors, but also between our countries.

Through my teaching job as a professor of theology and philosophy in universities in the United States and Austria, and with numerous Ambassadors for Peace around the world, we build bridges of reconciliation and dialogue in a spirit of understanding and service. Such work is necessary where there are tensions of race, religion, nationality and ethnic identity.

I assure you of our commitment to establish a world where our children and grandchildren will no longer have the separations that we have experienced but will live in a world full of mutual understanding and peace.

Dietrich Seidel, Ph.D.

It Happened to Me

It happened to me but it could happen to anyone who has convictions.

At the beginning of September 2012, I was in my French hometown, St. Jean de Maurienne. I visit this town, which is beautifully situated in the French Alps, nearly every other summer.

I was in a restaurant waiting for my husband to join me for lunch. I was shocked when the restaurant owner came to me holding the book, *Autobiography of Reverend Moon: My Life in Service to Peace*, up in the air and screaming in the direction of my table. I was just sitting at the table and he continued his expressive behavior, full of anger, ruthless and disrespectful, being upset and lifting up the book in disbelief.

There were many customers in the packed restaurant who could be part of this controversy. He said to me that he does not want such people in his restaurant. I asked him why not, and if his restaurant was open only for Catholics. He was too angry and agitated to have a normal conversation, and on the verge of becoming violent. I had to leave.

This is a restaurant I used to frequent quite often as it is close to my mother's apartment. In fact, during my previous visit there I met Mme Exartier, my friend, neighbor, and Ambassador for Peace. She told me that during the war she and her parents were hiding Jewish people and in this way saved many lives in my hometown. This was the reason that she was given the Ambassador for Peace award.

She was having lunch with three of her girlfriends at the next table. We had a lively conversation and I offered her the book, *Autobiography of Reverend Moon*, as a gift to her. All three of her friends became very excited and curious to read the book too. So I went to my car where I had other copies and gave them as gifts to the three ladies. Looking back, I believed one of them must have given one of the copies to the owner of the restaurant. She must have complained about the "secte Moon" as it is called by the newspapers.

I was not doing any propaganda activity, or entering the restaurant to give out the books. Quite the opposite. It was very natural, meeting my friend at the restaurant and her friends desired to have the books.

I sensed the irresponsibility of the media, driving public opinion to the point where there is a dangerous situation for religious freedom. The work for peace or any other ideal was diminished to zero because of the prejudice of the people.

The truth of the story was that I gave the book to Joe, one of our very dear friends from Savoie, when I met him at this restaurant. He was always so supportive of our events. He ended up calling me "*Marraine*" (Godmother). It made me feel so special every time he called me that. When we met him at that restaurant, he was very friendly, sharing his bottle of wine with us. How could we say no? In France that would be totally impolite. So, I gave him a copy of Father Moon's book "*Ma Vie au Service de la Paix*." He forgot it there in the restaurant, and when he went back to pick it up it was gone. So, I gave him another copy of the book.

Earlier, a few years before, I organized a benefit concert in my hometown of St. Jean de Maurienne on the anniversary of the day it was liberated from the war. The mayor gave us permission to use the public theater. We invested a lot of time to organize the event. Soon we realized the posters from the theater were being ripped down. The organizations supporting the event backed away, and the media started a barrage of negativity. They put up their own posters around town saying "Moonies behind the benefit concert."

It was extremely hurtful. People whom I knew were crossing the street to the other side trying not to encounter me. I felt the pain of Joan of Arc and all the lies against her when all she wanted was to save France. I was treated like her.

Still, I received encouraging words from the man who printed our flyers. He wrote a note: "Do not worry! I know all those who brainwashed people. I know all the bandits, the liars, the good for nothing people, they are all hiding in their offices. Keep doing what you are doing!"

True Love Will Prevail

This is my experience of true love and forgiveness. When we tried to organize an event not long ago, one of my friends caused it to be cancelled because of the connection to the Unification Church. I felt so betrayed by her.

Recently I met her at a picnic organized for the community. We first met briefly at the ticket counter. I was surprised and since she was busy talking with other people, I did not linger around her. For the whole meal I struggled so much because I still had so much hurt feelings from our last experience together, and I did not know how to handle the situation. For the whole meal she was speaking here and there and shaking hands, smiling and taking pictures and so on.

I was feeling so terrible and so low. I had to encourage myself. First, I had the feeling of no, no, no. After what happened last time there is no way I can go to her and say a few words. I am too much hurt. She broke my heart. She made the whole event crumble. She made a big mistake against True Parents and against me. How could she do that? She used to be my friend. I was getting nasty inside. But then I thought, am I not preaching love your enemy? But this time it does not apply, or does it? I just felt terrible.

How can I ever make it to accomplish anything? Who is on my side? Someday I feel I have nothing left, how can I go on. Is not Heaven on my side? Today does not look like it, sometimes it feels like Heaven is with everybody else but me. How can I forgive? My husband always forgave me. Forgiveness is a necessary daily bread. Suddenly I heard an inner voice: If I can forgive her, my Heavenly Father will too. So I started building new strength again to be able to love no matter what. And was not Dietrich telling me, I love you no matter what?

So, I picked up my purse and confidently walked toward her and said, "It is so very nice to see you again and how is your mom and your Dad?" She replied, "They are enjoying their retirement. I will tell them and my uncle too that we met. You know I am living with them. And three days a week I am staying in my office. I have a bed there and it is very convenient." And so on we talked. I was pleased to talk to her again. "Shall we make a picture together?" "Of course!"

Truly, true love will prevail.

Claiming Back my Hometown

After the passionate upheaval of last summer, when I organized a benefit concert in Savoie and received so much persecution, I visited several people in Montaimont while I was staying there for the summer. I brought Father Moon's autobiography as gifts.

I went to a pot luck dinner where people exchanged gifts. I left one copy of the autobiography of Reverend Moon on the table with the other gifts. As soon as the book was out, the atmosphere changed. My friend walked right up there and claimed the book, saying, "Oh, Reverend Moon? Yes, best seller in Korea. International best seller. You did not know?"

I visited another friend who loves music and dancing. Even though she is more than 90, at one of our reconciliation events she did sing and dance. Because of her age she is almost blind and cannot read, so I did not want to give her a book at first, just bringing her some sweets and drinking tea together.

After an hour I had to go and she said, "Do not go yet, stay a little longer. I never have any visits and I like you so much." After another half hour I said I had to go now. She said, "Please stay another 10 minutes." I did, drinking more tea. Then I said I really have to go now. She said, "Please do not go." So, I said, "Alright, since you cannot read and I wanted to give you a book to read, but I am sorry you can't so let's read together one chapter."

After one page: "Oh, que c'est beau, que c'est beau (how beautiful), continue." Another page: "Oh, que c'est beau, que c'est beau, continue." Another page: "I never heard such beautiful things before. Ma petite Betty, que tu es gentille, comme je t'aime, comme je t'aime." We both had tears in our eyes and I decided to come back after a few days to continue reading with her.

At the second visit her niece came saying, "No, no, no, no, no. You can't read this to my aunt. I know everything about Reverend Moon from television, and I do not want to have anything to do with him." I said, "I am so sorry you had to listen to the negative TV, but I am here to defend and clear the name of Reverend Moon in my country." She calmed down a little. She agreed to meet again at the church the next week.

A neighbor was happy to see me and said that she went to all our events in the past years; they were so special. "You are doing a wonderful job. Thanks for the book, and all my three friends want it too. Could you please dedicate it to them too? We want to stay in touch with you."

Another person said: "I can't believe how nasty those people were to you! I went to the theatre last September and was shocked it was closed. Thank you for the autobiography. I admire you. You are a fighter!"

Don't Worry, Be Happy, Mamas

> Written to Elisabeth by her daughter, Diesa, after an experience in which Elisabeth's loving kindness was rejected, causing her deep pain.

Hi Mamas,

We are at Big Bear Mountain now, about to go snowboarding...

I wanted to send you a short email to remind you to try not to worry, and to BE HAPPY.

I am so sorry that such people are still living and holding on to a lot of pain and resentment. And I am so sorry that you are also in pain from it.

They say, "Hurt people, hurt people."

But then the opposite must also be true... "Loved people, love people."

So, let's just do our best to love our hearts out! If we succumb to the emotional attacks of others, then we lower our spiritual frequencies to theirs. BUT, if our love can be STRONGER than the pain of others, then it will surely, slowly, take over all the pain, until there is only love and happiness left.

F.A.I.T.H. = Feel As If iT Happened!

Anytime you have a sad feeling, think of THREE happy things that bring joy to your heart.

Yesterday was 95% super nice, fun, and happy!! Wow! That's pretty good!!

I love you, Mamas! You are my one and only Mamas! And I will always be here for you.

(And Dadas too... maybe you can hear his voice in my message?)

Remember, to always have sunshine in your heart!

Servus and Bussi!!

Love,

Diesa

Ecumenical Work

The following entries reveal more of Elisabeth's desire to work together with people of all faiths and backgrounds.

The first recounts some experiences at the restaurant in Vienna owned by one of Dietrich's students. Here they invited guests to share a meal and their hearts. This laid the foundation for further ecumenical work in Vienna

One such effort was with a Syrian Orthodox Church. The second entry is a prayer offered on the occasion of Dietrich's 70th birthday, together with their Syrian friends.

Another entry is the prayer offered by Elisabeth while back in the United States. This was part of an interfaith petition for the healing of America.

Finally, Elisabeth reports on the day she attended the special Mass at her grandfather's church, Chapelle Sainte Marguerite. Such a small church is unable to host all those who attend this annual event, and so they gather outside, enjoying the beauty of nature, high in the French Alps. Elisabeth is well known to the priest, and had an inspiring experience meeting him after the service, as well as all the attendees.

At the Shooters Restaurant

Spetim Redo was my husband's student in his World Religions class at Webster University in Vienna, where he is studying diplomacy. He and his wife, Claudiana, are from Albania. He has a dream to become the president of his country.

He owns a restaurant in Vienna called Shooters, close to the American Embassy and the university. He invited us to have dinner at his restaurant. We had deep sharing. Before leaving, we held hands and prayed for the realization of his dream. That was in 2008. Spetim said he remembers my prayer.

Spetim and Claudiana Redo, with Dr. Stephan Sacu, receiving Ambassador for Peace awards at the Shooters Restaurant

We invited many guests for dinner at the Shooters restaurant, and over the months we started giving

Ambassadors for Peace awards. Last week we had such a meeting with a few people. Over the meal we shared close bonds.

Dr. Kasiri, who wrote his Ph.D. thesis about Islam and Christianity, said that after the preceding meeting he looked upon his family with new eyes.

Over the years we went back to our hometowns many times and appointed many Ambassadors for Peace, often at this Shooters Restaurant. We worked also with the Syrian Orthodox Church in Vienna, where we held benefit concerts for the Syrian refugees.

September 2013 Prayer on the Occasion of Dietrich's 70th Birthday, with our Syrian Friends in Vienna

To our Beloved God, our Heavenly Parent,

Today as we look back on our 70 years of life, we are grateful that you sustained us. You were with us in time of joy and time of hope and you were especially with us in time of trial and difficulty.

When we could not walk you took us on your back, when we were in the dark, you showed us the light.

And today again we offer our life to you, and gratitude to be alive. We give you thanks and praise you.

May our life be worthy in your eyes.

Today as the whole world is on flames and ready to burst at any moment and any place, we look up to you, keeping our faces toward heaven, looking for guidance and direction.

More than politics, you are the leading force, the love that wins over evil. The love that can forgive, and bring the peaceful ideal loving world that humankind is waiting for.

Today we are specially thinking of our brothers and sisters in miserable situations, who suffer from hunger, persecution and war time.

The divine providence that you are directing will prevail and your peaceful ideal world will come to exist. You always send prophets in those times, you sent our Joan of Arc in France, Gandhi in India, Martin Luther King in the U.S., and Reverend Sun Myung Moon in Korea.

Please dry the tears of your children, as it is said in the Last Days you would. May we be able to forgive our enemies.

At the Syrian Orthodox Church in Vienna

May you shower Syria with your true love and bestow great blessing upon this nation. We are truly all brothers and sisters, and may our work for peace bring harmony upon all religions.

This we pray in the name of Jesus, Reverend Moon, the True Parent of Heaven, Earth and Humankind, the names of all the saints, and in our own names, Dietrich and Elisabeth Seidel.

Petition to Heaven

> Elisabeth's prayer at the "Petition to Heaven" interfaith prayer call, October 14, 2016

Dear God,

You are the invisible Heavenly Parent who loves everyone. Today is the first day of our interfaith prayer call to heal the nation. Please accept our request.

We are so grateful that we can live here in America, the land of the free, true land of the brave. You have given us plenty. May America fulfill its destiny to serve and protect the world. May all churches in America come to unity that is acceptable to You. You are so great and large, You can go beyond denominations; in fact You created us, so You are our Heavenly Father and Mother and Your heart is like a parent who wants to gather all Your children, including the prodigal sons and daughters. May we hear Your voice in our hearts, where You reside in the core of our hearts.

Today we want to truly repent for America, this land that we love. We are so sorry that sin is still rampant, that we criticize and reject each other, that we did not love our neighbor enough. We are truly sorry, Heavenly Parent. We love You. Please forgive us.

Most of all, we pray that with Your love and Your presence with us, that all evils will diminish and finally disappear with the coming of Your Kingdom, where every one of us can live with You and with each other as an extended family. We pray for the protection of the family as You created it.

How sorrowful is Your heart to see the misuse of love everywhere. We are sorry for all the addictions of all sorts. We repent for that, that we let it go without doing enough. Healing America will also heal our families.

We are called by Your name, so we want to work for You, to be an extension for You, and we want to take responsibility. May You heal this land and hear our prayer.

I pray all this in the name of Jesus, all the saints, the True Parents, and my own name. Amen.

Chapelle Sainte Marguerite

The first time we conducted the Holy Marriage Blessing in a church was unexpected even to me, completely out of the blue. It was at Chapelle Sainte Marguerite by Montaimont, the church of my Grandfather Jules.

Once a year in August, when the weather is warm high in the French Alps, Christians gather outside with Père Durieux, because the chapel is too small. In front, about 50 to 70 chairs are set up, and others stand or sit on the grass.

Before our visits to our hometowns in France and Austria, we were at East Garden where Father was saying, who has holy wine in their purse? Show me your holy wine in your purse. He then repeated: "You should always have holy wine in your purse." That Sunday by beautiful Chapelle Sainte Marguerite, I had holy wine in my purse in a small bottle.

The priest, Père Durieux, by now is my very good friend. Shortly before the service ended, a very strong idea popped into my mind – holy wine. Do it now. But how?

At the Chapelle Sainte Marguerite

After the service people are in no hurry to go because the surroundings are so magnificent, so I walked to the priest and put a dollar coin in his hand. I said: "A token from the USA for you, *In God We Trust* is written on the coin. Besides, I also have holy wine for you because we believe in family values, in fidelity, in waiting for marriage before having sex and telling everyone about it. Open your hand that now you can receive some holy wine from America." He did.

Then I walked to the mayor, who was listening to our conversation, and she also took holy wine. Then it was like the spirit world was opening up and everyone received holy wine. Later on that day I went around in the area where there was a celebration with music, and a picnic with wine and cheese, and everyone that day received free holy wine.

Restoration of Beloved France

As the readers should now be well aware, Elisabeth's love for her home country of France is very deep. Even though she had so many difficult experiences returning to her hometown, the majestic mountains still move her heart and warm her soul.

The first entry here shows her passion for her beloved France. Reflecting on the life, and tragic death of Jeanne d'Arc (Joan of Arc) and of others accused of heresy, she shares her determination to seek justice, reconciliation and peace, never letting race or religion divide us.

The other entries describe the efforts made by Elisabeth and others to guide France to play a part in creating the longed-for world of peace. The second entry here explains how a small group created a Holy Ground in Savoie, to provide spiritual support for this process.

Unfortunately, the path has been tortuous, fraught with many difficulties. The next entry is a letter she wrote to a friend, responding to his struggles and sharing her own. Despite these challenges, Elisabeth encourages her friend to have faith and keep persevering, as she does.

The final entries are tributes to two of the earliest Unification members in France, written by Elisabeth when they ascended to the spiritual realm. Both were instrumental in welcoming Elisabeth into the French "family" and teaching and guiding her in her early years, with deepest love. We feel Elisabeth's eternal gratitude to them for the sacrifices they made for the sake of her beloved France.

Where Is France Going?

When I was a child at the elementary school in La Chambre, learning my history lessons by heart, there was a fact which disturbed me: "*La nuit de la Saint Barthélemy*" (the St. Bartholomew's Day massacre). On this painful night many were killed because of their beliefs, making them heretics in the eyes of the Catholics.

At that time, still a child of 8 or 10, I already had a passion for justice, reconciliation and peace. I wanted to work to prevent those kinds of situations happening again.

In the memories of my youth I was pondering why in beautiful France, the country of my birth, why those things could happen. Do we not have the motto, "*Liberté, égalité, fraternité*"?

I wanted to get out of my mountains, as maybe the high summits were blocking my view and I wanted to see further. My first stop was Switzerland, then England where I stayed for two years as a French assistant in a middle and high school.

I realized what they were teaching there concerning Jeanne d'Arc was very different from what they were teaching in the French schools. In my French school, my teacher told me, and it was written in my history book, that the English burned Jeanne d'Arc alive! In England we learned that the French bishops burned Joan of Arc.

It is very important to have freedom of religion and freedom of thought. A war between Muslims and Christians would be more devastating than any other war. Did we forget the Jewish persecution during World War II?

I married a man of Austrian-German descent, Dr. Dietrich Seidel, a scientist and theologian. In accordance with the vow made in my childhood, we worked to reconcile religions with bridges of love and dialogue. Our motto: "We are all brothers and sisters under ONE GOD."

Love for others goes before my religion. Our holy marriage signifies a marriage of peace between our nations France-Austria-Germany, that never wars will come again, but, instead, a world of love that we have all been waiting for.

Holy Ground in Savoie

On September 7, 2014 at 7 pm, four people established a new Holy Ground for Savoie in the French Alps at the Chapelle de St. Marguerite. Jean Paul Chaudy, Michel Detaille, Dietrich and Elisabeth Seidel drove to the chapel, which is situated above Lac du Loup at an altitude of 1650 meters. Jean Paul and Elisabeth have ancestors in the nearby villages of Bonvillard and Montaimont. From the Col de la Madeleine, which is close to the chapel, one can see Mont Blanc and also the valleys of Tarantaise and Maurienne.

The chapel is shown (top right) in this postcard from Montaimont

After an introductory prayer from Elisabeth Seidel, in which she mentioned the restoration of Savoie and an open heart of the people towards God's providence and our True Parents, Jean Paul holy salted the four corners of the chapel. He conducted the Holy Ground ceremony, by putting some earth from the Holy Ground in Lyon at the four corners and then inside the chapel. The four people positioned themselves at the four corners of the chapel, to protect the building and that only good spirits from the spirit world and angelic beings may have access to the new Holy Ground.

The chapel, representing Christianity, is symbolic for the restoration and the faith of the people of Savoie. The ceremony concluded with Jean Paul taking pictures and meeting two nearby farmers, who were representative of all the people who seek full salvation by supporting our True Parents. May this new Holy Ground fulfill its purpose of sincere prayers and spiritual conditions.

Letter to My Friend in Lyon

Thank you for sharing your letter to True Mother. I remember when Father was in Danbury, he asked the members to send him their testimonies.[27] I remember it being a liberating experience, and thinking what else we need to accomplish. It seems that you give yourself the answers in your letter to True Mother.

I remember leaders having difficulties with their children. When they asked True Mother, she said that you must trust that God will guide them (your children).

Every morning I pray with so much tears about so many different situations all over the world, and in particular in my own family. One sentence from True Father always come to my mind: What comes to our Blessed Families has to be restored in the world through us.

I hope, like you, that victory will come at the end. Did not Reiner Vincenz, the spiritual father of France, say that we must overcome everything until the end?

We always hope, always have faith, and always love.

---

[27] Elisabeth's Letter to Father Moon is included in the earlier section of this book entitled "In Canada."

Thinking of beloved Lyon, where you have been the spiritual father for so long, with the help of so many saints from spiritual world, the victory is near. I feel it. I sense it.

We left God with tears, and we return to God with tears. Soon it will be heavenly Lyon, and heavenly France, even heavenly St. Jean de Maurienne.

Every day I call on Mary and Elisabeth and Zechariah and Jesus and John the Baptist, the patron saint of St. Jean, my hometown (can you imagine). People have been telling me they saw the Virgin Mary; they went to Lourdes. One friend made the vow to go to Lourdes 18 times, the number of times that Mary appeared there. They give me pens from Lourdes and Chappellet, and pictures and holy water. Mother said Europe is so important for Christianity.

In the meantime, I am roaming around St. Jean every day trying to make a difference, waiting for a miracle.

Even for the most difficult town in the whole wide world, God must have a way. Today they are celebrating the Fête of Saint Jean Baptiste and I truly feel so sorry for him that he could not bear witness to Jesus. I hope he too will receive the Holy Marriage Blessing.

I often meet Arlette, and friends of Arlette too. We had a meal together. One friend tells me every time I meet her that she will remember our benefit concert all her life. She liked it so much. It was so high spirited, and beautiful, and something for the heart. She felt truly sorry that we were forbidden access to the public theater in St. Jean due to the negative media.

Another friend, Catherine, also invited me for dinner and invited friends she wanted me to meet. The whole evening we talked, and they asked a lot of questions. Her son was furious about religion, but we had a lovely evening and I will meet them again before my departure.

It is very slow, and indirect, but this is what it is. At the same time, I give you some insights from my hometown. I have been fortunate to have my beloved husband with me here from the spiritual world, helping with the contacts and supporting me.

Thank you so much for sharing your heart with True Mother. I truly could see myself in the same shoes.

May God bless you always. One of your grandchildren may become a very important and providential figure for France. God bless you. Warm greetings, Elisabeth

Tribute to Bernadette Bellay Sattlberger

> On the occasion of Bernadette's passing to the spiritual world, Elisabeth wrote this beautiful tribute to her dear friend and eternal spiritual sister, with whom she pioneered witnessing in Bordeaux – with those special shoes Father Moon bought for her.

Dear Bernadette,

Thank you for being our beloved elder French sister. I miss you already!

Your deep wisdom, your heart of gold, but most of all, you were the smartest and most intelligent sister.

You did not talk too much, but whatever you said made so much sense, so much logic, that you could persuade so many French brothers and sisters in the old days, explaining why the Divine Principle is true, why it is the new revelation of our age, and could convince them in any heated discussions.

You were the one who opened the door one night as I knocked at the Paris Headquarters on December 1970.

I was with you in Bordeaux pioneering this city together first with Michel Ferrant. One of the first things I remember is you put all of us on white rice for seven days kind of fast, and I did not like this condition. So, we had our first taste of a Cain and Abel situation, struggled all we could, till there was nothing else but spiritual children starting to come.

You were so instrumental for so many brothers and sisters who joined our movement at that time. We had many fierce battles, and you always came out victorious. All these beautiful people like Jean Pierre Gabriel, who went away for 40 days to study and came back and joined. As well as Christiane Coste, Monique Rabat, Michel Bredard, Marie Thérèse Agat, Josianne Fredoux, Bernard Delahaye, Michelle Elkaim, and others. Those people were somehow the pillars of our movement in France. You were aware of each one's situation and needs, and because of you we could be victorious in Bordeaux. One day France will recognize you.

Finally, last but not least, you found your true love in Austria, with Kurt your awesome husband and best friend, and your two fantastic kids.

Bernadette, you could unite faith and intellect. Bravo, Bernadette we love you.

Thank you for the last summer party at your home by Linz. You made a delicious luncheon for all of us. For me it was like a good bye party, but *ce n'est qu'un au revoir, ma soeur*. On another day we all meet again at your new beautiful home in heaven where we will have so many joyful luncheons and get together again and again.

Bernadette (center with glasses) with Elisabeth and other French Unificationists

Take care, Bernadette, and safe passage to you. Your eternal sister, Elisabeth

Eternal Father of France

> Written when Reiner Vincenz was suffering ill health in his last years on earth

Dearest Reiner,

Wishing you a recovery for good health, strength, energy and love. May you feel the love and eternal gratitude of all those to whom you have given new life, saving them from darkness.

Truly you are the only one that God trusted to come to France and bring the news of True Parents to this most rebellious country. Only you could do it. So many brothers and sisters are eternally grateful to you.

Reiner Vincenz (center) with early members in France, Henri Blanchard (right) and Armand Dano (back)

You paid so much indemnity and sacrificed all. The early days are forever engraved in our heart and mind. Only you could speak to the people of our nation with such faith and conviction, restoring all animosity between Germany and France, and breathing the love of God and True Parents in the early members.

I know because of you, my faith never vacillated for these last 40 years. When in difficulty, I thought of what you said and this kept me going.

So many times, I met brothers and sisters from all nations on whom you made great impact, and because of you they too kept going. Is it not what you used to say: "The one who overcomes everything will arrive at the end"?

Please be well and please be peaceful. We send also much love to Barbara, your daughter, and very special grandkids.

With our prayers and love, Elisabeth Seidel

Reflections on the Life of Reiner Vincenz

Written by Elisabeth when he passed away in July 2014

Reiner Vincenz is the spiritual father of France. He loved France and each member with the immense love of our True Parents. Each day, his only conversation was about our Heavenly Father, the True Parents, and the situation of each brother and sister. His love was constant, never vacillating, never changing. He raised France with this heart and educated the members with German rigor.

He saved brothers and sisters from so many ferocious spiritual attacks. These attacks were all there, but they were invisible, subtle and mortal, spiritually and sometimes physically. Reiner knocked them out, one by one, in order to save my country, together with a bunch of youngsters for whom he invested his whole life.

This was Paris in the early seventies, when the Church Headquarters was situated on "Rue le Sueur" (Road of Sweat). This said it all. The few of us still here today in 2014 sometimes wonder how we survived this time. Truly without Reiner we could not have done it. He tried very hard to understand each single person and how the spirit of French people works in order to love them.

Reiner and Barbara Vincenz, with their infant daughter, Leena

He came from Germany the enemy of France, and he had to reverse this situation, to be the one who could love France the most. In my opinion, he did it. And I do not know of anybody else who could give new life to France in the place of the True Parents.

Living with God

I gave this collection the title "Living with God" as each entry, whether it be a reflection, a poem or a report, describes living a life with God as one's center and guiding presence. This is surely the message Dietrich embodied in his life of faith, and Elisabeth's writings share this same heart.

Examples of living with God appear in the very first article, "I Knew God Must Exist," where she traces her life of faith from its beginnings where she was forbidden to even enter a church to her concluding prayer that everyone be embraced by God's love. They continue through her discussion of the meaning of Christmas, from her childhood memories of gifts and festive decorations to her current experiences and hopes for interfaith harmony.

While living with God can be uplifting and inspiring, it can also take the form of comfort during the most difficult and challenging times of one's life. As we read more reflections here, we can understand how Elisabeth appreciates the presence of God, either directly, or more often, through other people.

The final entry encourages us to start the day well, preparing both body and spirit, communing with God to gain energy and guidance for the day. Then the day includes God, from start to finish. And this God is the all-embracing God who loves His children, no matter who they are, and who encourages us, likewise, to love each other.

I Knew God Must Exist

One thing I remember from my childhood was my Dad's attitude towards the church. He forbade me to go to church while I was growing up, saying that I can choose my own religion as an adult. Later I found out that he was not happy with the Catholic Church after a bad experience with a priest.

Of course, I started being very inquisitive and curious about my situation, that I was not allowed to even enter the church in my small hometown. I was envious of my friends who were learning about the Bible and religious teachings.

When I was about 20 years of age, I did have many questions about God and why there was evil in the world. Does God really exist, and where can I find the loving God? I started traveling to Greece, England and Italy looking for truth.

Indeed, God was leading me in His own way. When I saw the beauty of the Greek countryside and the islands with their surrounding blue and green sea, the clear skies, the bright sun and all the happy people I met, I knew that God is alive. He simply must exist.

When I arrived in Italy, I was sharing an apartment with a Catholic sister who had left her order. She told me that she knew someone who could answer all my questions. Eventually, I met this group of people and I did study with them. One by one, God gave me answers to all these questions I had stored up in my heart. I felt there was a lot of spiritual guidance from angels and some of my good ancestors, especially from my Grandma Marie. This was for me a time of enormous spiritual growth and transformation. It was clear to me that a lasting peaceful world can only be built on God's love and that my first step towards that goal consists of building a God-loving family.

Soon I went to Paris and decided to work with all my heart, my love, my youth and my enthusiasm for God and a new world to come. This time, being the age of Aquarius, is filled with expectation for the arrival of a new master who will come for all religions. Some may expect the return of Buddha, or the return of Muhammad, while others expect Christ to return or, like people in the East, are hoping for the arrival of the True Man. I worked hard with little tangible results but with increasing internal rewards. I tried to live for the sake of others, finding it quite difficult. However, the loving God sustained me.

In 1977, I married Dietrich, who is of German-Austrian descent. We felt called to allow our love to heal our nations from past resentments and hurts.

We also were involved in reaching out to people of different faiths, feeling that God's heart is too big to love only one particular faith. In this way, I want to contribute to world peace and God's coming kingdom on earth. I pray for everyone to be part of it.

Meaning of Christmas

When I was a child, we put our shoes under the Christmas tree to receive presents. There were two small stores in my Alpine village that carried toys. During the Christmas season, going and coming from school I was spellbound by the festive colors and glitter emanating from these stores. It was such a time of expectancy and joy. On Christmas morning we were usually given oranges and "*papillottes*" (chocolate candy wrapped in gold, silver or colored paper) together with a small present.

Now, for me, the meaning of Christmas is also a time of expectation and joy, for Christ to come with all the spiritual masters bringing us together from all faiths, reaching out for each other with a heart of love. Somehow, I know Christ and the spiritual masters are not only in our hearts but are walking with us on earth assisting us to do good, to love for the sake of others and to become Ambassadors for Peace.

For a long time, I have been welcoming the New Year at midnight with prayer, not only for a fulfilling and spiritually rewarding year but also for a world of peace and God-loving families. I think it is important how we start our day, week or year. Starting with God will give us spiritual protection, guidance and power for living a meaningful life.

I am so happy that during our short stay in San Diego we met with Fozia from the religion of Islam – we always pray together. When we do so, I feel Jesus and Muhammad are brothers in the spirit world after loving each other as Fozia and I love each other here on earth.

Christmas Visit

I had a visit from above, from two magnificent birds in my backyard. They stayed on the tree for about half an hour enjoying the sun in the freezing northeast weather. I think they were pheasants.

I admired their beauty, their color and their attitude to make my backyard their new home. After half an hour they flew away, parading their wings with blue, yellow and orange, looking at me like they needed adoption or something.

This morning they came back. I could not believe they came back.

If they come back again, I will give them names and they will be my new pets. How beautiful is God's creation. Halifax and Margot. They came back.

Healing Power

Last year over Christmas, 2008, my husband Dietrich was in the hospital. I had a lot of "blues" at that time, worrying about his recovery. I was feeling desperate, lonely and forgotten.

One evening, after coming home from the hospital, I remember turning on the TV in a state of hopelessness. I ended up watching CNN. Totally unexpectedly there was a show "CNN Heroes of the Year" that moved me to tears. In fact, after the presentation of each hero, I could not help crying when I realized how much one enthusiastic person with a dedicated heart can do. It picked me up, made me feel uplifted, and inspired me more than any other show I ever watched in my life.

There was a girl who set up the program "Back on Your Feet" for homeless people and drug addicts. She made them run every morning so that they could have a new spirit. This way some of them found healing in their situation. There was a lady who organized women to rebuild each other's homes with volunteers after they had collapsed during Hurricane Katrina. There was a lady who opened schools in Africa for special needs girls, and so on.

At that time, my daughter was in Israel, Jordan and Palestine conducting an empowerment program for young women and to bring a measure of peace in the midst of the turmoil of war.

During these days it was comforting to receive phone calls from both of my children, Christopher and Diesa. As I was calling Diesa one evening, sobbing about my husband's situation and hearing about her escape from war-torn Palestine, she became my personal hero. She said: "If you think and believe Dad will be better, he will." Then she fasted seven single days for her Dad's complete recovery. The seventh day of her fast, two of her best friends joined in the fast.

The same evening of the last day of the fast my husband experienced total recovery – that was the evening of New Year's Day. It was like a miracle to feel God's love and healing power through Diesa and her two special friends. I will never forget that.

Isolation Is Hell

I was reading "Heaven and the Afterlife," true stories from people who have glimpsed the world beyond. It was written by Jim Garlow, senior pastor of Skyline Church in San Diego, and Keith Wall, a publishing veteran.

One of the last stories in this book talked about an encounter in hell experienced by David Rutherford. As David was at the doctor's office to be treated for pleurisy, the doctor gave him a shot and he fainted. During this short time until the nurses revived him back to consciousness, he went with his spirit to a frightening place that he called hell. He said: "It was the most agonizing experience of my life. I felt incredibly isolated and alone like there was not the slightest chance of belonging, or ever being cared for again. It was absolutely excruciating."

David said he struggled over the next few days to understand why his experience has been so terrifying. Slowly he realized that God had given him a vision – a minuscule snapshot – of what hell is really like. He knows now, first hand, that it is a place of absolute and complete loneliness, a desperate isolation that no one ever experiences here on earth, no matter how alone they think they are.

David did not just feel separated from God – a state that many people might associate with being in hell. He was cut off from everyone and everything familiar and comforting. Of the hundreds of faces racing past him, not one offered him the slightest morsel of connection or contact.

He also said: "People joke about preferring to go to hell because that's where all their friends will be or that is where the party is." But he said what he saw made him realize it is not like that at all. No matter where you go on earth you have something in common with people, it is possible to connect and communicate on a basic level. Not in hell. It is a horrible feeling.

David went on to becomes a full-time pastor in Fresno California, and his ministry is shaped with an extraordinary empathy toward people who feel alone in the world. He knows that the search for connection with each of them drives people far more than theology.

I myself also believe that people can die in isolation or loneliness. If a baby does not receive love, is left alone, he or she can die.

It is our mandate as human beings to reach out to each other, especially the Christian churches, who preach "love your neighbor as yourself," and especially us in the Unification community, who preach "Let's love with true love, and a parental heart."

If I know of someone with a difficult situation, my responsibility is involved, no matter how busy I am. In extreme cases, if I cannot take responsibility, then I have to find someone in my place. Taking care of each other, this is how I see the Kingdom of Heaven.

If this person is me, then I have to say, "Please help me, I cannot make it alone." If there are true brothers and sisters, which I think there are, then their hands will be within reach.

And if this does not work, then we can stay all alone and eat chocolates.

Evergreens by My House

Hoflein, Austria, March 13, 2009

There are evergreens all around me, by the snow mountain.
Early morning running to the forest.
Pledging to God.
As owners of the eternal peaceful world to come.
In deep winter there are evergreens all around me.
Fertile soil where healing volcanoes' water runs.
Deep underneath making everlasting green healthy trees.
Beyond calm there is God.
Sending prayers to Heaven.
Wishes and requests.
Delivered by my angels.
God drying my tears,
There. In the woods among my peaceful trees.
They give me hope, comfort and love.
There the atmosphere is beyond calm.
Sending prayers carried by my angels.
Beautiful evergreens by my home.
I am waiting for my son
To come home again.

The Woman Who Knew the Taste of God's Tears

Once upon a time there was a woman whose only desire was to do the will of God.

At one point in her life, everything started crumbling down out of nowhere, one upon the other.

The same year she lost both her father and mother. A few days after her mom passed away, her beloved only brother said: Now I want to cut all bridges with you.

She shed a few tears and continued on her way.

When she was getting up to pray, tears came to her eyes, she had nothing to say. But she prayed.

At a difficult time, her husband had a stroke and while still at the hospital, her daughter was in a devastating earthquake in a place far away. For 24 hours she had no news if the daughter was alive or dead. The woman could only pray and cry. Then cry and pray. By a miracle the daughter was alive.

One day the love of her life passed away. The woman could only cry and pray. Then pray and cry. This very day someone told her, get out of my house.

She took a plane to go bury her husband. But no one sat by her in the lonely plane. Not even her kids. They were also suffering with their own pain and could not comfort anyone. The woman shed bitter tears, traumatized by the earlier weeks of her beloved suffering. Wounded, dazed, thunderstruck, she experienced Jesus on the cross.

Will I find my way, she thought?

She did and continued on her way.

When she arrived home, she realized her previous tenant was taking her to court, and the new tenant was on drugs. Both of them decided to take her to court. All hell was breaking loose. There was 10,000 dollars to pay for the lawyer and repairs in the house.

The woman shed more tears, and could not pay her taxes. She just prayed, trying to love the enemy.

Soon she thought, I could be ejected from my home, and perhaps I could end up living under a bridge. It scared the hell out of her. There were no days without tears.

Her eyes were always damp.

The dampness of her eyes was mixing with the dampness of God's tears, like a mystical place, and a love for God that nothing could take away anymore.

When the love of God reunited with His children is that strong, the Fall will never be possible anymore.

This is how miserable God was, and how joyful He is finding again His children.

The way of the woman is directed toward the Kingdom of God, where she will arrive one day pretty soon after overcoming all the tribulations.

The Geese – Why We Should Learn from Them

The geese fly high, happy and free, changing the ones who fly first now and then so that no-one becomes too exhausted. If one is not well or can't go on flying and drops to the ground, two geese will automatically go with her to the ground and stay there till she is totally recovered.

Me too, I dropped to the ground and deeper after my husband passed. I am so grateful to two persons who stayed with me till I recovered.

One is my friend Traudl, who was checking on me regularly. Totally unselfishly she would pick me up in the morning on her way to work, drop me off at the library or in town, and pick me up for lunch. Many times, we would share breakfast or lunch together and dinner too, and have talk therapy.

The second one is Jenny. We worked together one day a week or more to publish my husband's writings. She was also there for me, to protect me from any attack coming at me. I was picked up at the airport, and a bag of groceries was ready for my fridge. She unselfishly did all the computer work needing to be done. She was only one phone call away, and would come running if any emergency occurred.

Another person was Irene with whom I prayed together over the phone. During this period of time we prayed for America, for President Trump and his administration, for the young people of this country, for God to stay in America, for all the abusive relationships to be transformed into healthy relationships. This gave me a point during the day to structure my day and not fall into despair.

So, the conclusion is for pastors who oversee their congregation: Make sure everyone is taken care of. Sometimes it is needed to ask if no-one is volunteering. I know of one friend in Europe who also lost her husband. She did not pick up her phone, and she went to the grave every day, on her own, secluded, shedding tears, not knowing the way out.

In the Kingdom of God which we are building, no such situation should exist. God will wipe away every tear through us who are His arms and hands to reach out to others.

How We Start our Day Sets the Tone for the Whole Day

The first thing I like to do is brush my teeth and drink a glass of water. But when my husband was here, his first thoughts were always for God, our Heavenly Parent. Before he got out of bed he would pause in short prayer and meditation. Then the day could start.

Then, it was like 10-minute sessions for different things like shower and get dressed, 10 minutes of exercises for me, 10 minutes for cleaning up and making breakfast. Then reading spiritual texts before eating.

Many times, Dietrich would start reading while I was still cleaning up. I always like a clean environment around me. It helps bring good vibrations and good thoughts. Beauty is uplifting to the mind, so the reading brings more good thoughts and more good vibes and energy. If you are still in a fuzzy and sleepy state it wakes you up to a good mood and to a good day.

Ideally, we recommend one hour. Sometimes we had to shorten it depending on our schedule. But we never liked to miss it, because it was setting the tone for the day. It gives our spirit the elements it needs to grow and to enter the day with love and discipline.

We did not like to leave home also without prayer and discipline. Then we would continue our prayers in the car going places, or put on a cd with inspirational words. These habits gave us protection and guidance from God, and sharing our deepest hearts and longing with our Heavenly Parent as well as comforting Him/Her, and loving each other, the three of us.

If we took a walk we always started with a prayer, actually we used to call it a prayer walk, to clear our minds and pause to know where we are at, and which direction to continue. When we traveled in the car with our children, they also heard our prayers.

Looking back all the places we were, we spread prayers everywhere. It says in the Bible to pray without ceasing.

Dietrich was always ready to pray till the end. When he had long stays at the hospital, I always called him first thing in the morning before I ate breakfast. Sometimes I was on a morning prayer walk and talking together with God was refreshing. This again was setting the tone for the day.

After Dietrich passed, I was moved to tears to hear that his friend Stephan in San Diego prays for him every Wednesday. He said that is Dietrich's day, as each day he prays for someone or something.

Stephan and friends and neighbors were all invited for Dietrich's last birthday on earth and they signed a booklet. After they left, Dietrich wrote: "These are all God's children."

Indeed, we are all God's children.

Help from Heaven

We have often heard of people who recognize signs from Heaven in a penny found unexpectedly, or a whiff of a loved one's perfume long after they have passed over, or finding something that was long forgotten at just the right moment, or perhaps a dream that encourages and inspires at a challenging time in one's life. These may be interpreted as the involvement of angels in our lives, or the presence of the spirits of our loved ones, or simply God finding a way to guide us if we are open to it.

In these entries, Elisabeth tells of several such instances where she experienced the presence of heavenly beings, or guidance from above.

How inspiring it was for her to find an inn that bore the name of her town in France where she was born, and to discover its history. Such a moment provided comfort and encouragement in her efforts to bring people of all faiths together harmoniously.

As she already recounted in earlier entries, Elisabeth was involved in a serious accident prior to being introduced to her future husband, Dietrich, but her injuries, which could have been fatal, although serious were relatively minor and she made a full recovery. At that time she felt the presence of God protecting her, and witnesses told her they saw Jesus and angels with her preventing the car from crushing her. Here we learn that this was not the only time she received help from the angels, protecting and healing both her physical body and that of her beloved Dietrich.

The final entry contains Elisabeth's personal experiences of pennies from heaven, and other such signs of encouragement and God's love.

God's Blessings Come in Unexpected Ways

I come from the country of Joan of Arc and Bernadette Soubirous, the country with the French Revolution as well as the country where St Genevieve, Patron Saint of Paris, was praying so hard to save the French capital from the Huns. Truly France had a spiritual mission, and she still has.

I was born in Chambery, France. When I and some friends were visiting ministers in the area of Stockbridge, Great Barrington and South Lee in Massachusetts, I came across a beautiful bed and breakfast called "The Chambery Inn." I was very intrigued to see such a sumptuous house named after my small hometown.[28] I learned that nuns from Chambery came to South Lee as missionaries and founded a Catholic school. The Inn is the remnant of this school.

Here I was in the same area finishing the work of my beloved sister nuns. My spiritual goal is working for reconciliation and cooperation among the existing churches. Like Joan and Bernadette and Genevieve, and my beloved Chambery sisters, I too heard the voice of God in my heart pushing me to go beyond race, nation and denomination, because now is the time for God's love to embrace, love, heal, forgive, renew all humankind with a new message.

Sometimes I feel so close to my special French friends because, like them, over the years I tasted rejection and misunderstanding. I remember a song that my friend sang at my birthday party, with the words "I look up, I put my eyes toward heaven to hide my tears." And with that feeling,

---

[28] Elisabeth wrote in her autobiography that she has three hometowns: Chambery, the capital of Savoie, where she was born; La Chambre, a village where she spent her childhood, and St. Jean de Maurienne, a larger town where she went to high school.

before there are more tears, I knock at the minister's door. Please, Heaven, hear my prayer soaked with tears, and please Mrs. Minister do not close your door on me. Do not be in the middle of something, too busy to welcome me.

As it is said in the Bible, knock and it will be opened. Because God's blessings always come in the most unexpected way.

Angels' Help

When I was a child, I visited my Aunt Yvonne often. I liked her, and she loved me back. When I was around 5 or 6 years of age, I remember talking with her about angels.

She said everyone has a guardian angel. She had a huge picture in her bedroom of one angel with wings, overlooking a child and protecting him as he was playing by the water. I remember this picture as it if it was yesterday. Although I was still a child, this thought stayed with me that I was protected by my guardian angel.

About a month before I was going to get married, I almost lost my life, and my life was given back to me. As I was crossing the street, rushing before the red light, a car hit me in the back full speed and I fell on the ground. Before I could realize what was happening, I was between the four wheels of the car which was rolling over me. In a spilt second I said, "Heavenly Father my life is for you." The car somehow was lifted up in special places in order not to crush me. I remember it was like legions of angels loving me and protecting me and saving me.

Besides a broken arm and some internal injuries which healed I was fine. I did not even bring the driver to court. I was so pleased to have my life back.

Another time I had an experience of angels was when I went to see a chiropractor to fix my back. After the treatment, he told me that it was the first time he saw so many angels entering the room, and that it was an honor that he could heal me with the help of the angels.

The conclusion is that angels are messengers of God and are here to help each one of us to make our life more successful and more loving. We just need to learn how to communicate with them.

Dreams and Angels in Our Life Again

My husband had a stroke at the end of December, 2009, while we were in Austria. It was a lot of stress for him and for me. All of a sudden, our lives were turned around and most things we took for granted became an ordeal. How to remember things, and how to do simple things became complicated. Like to take a shower, to eat breakfast, to get dressed and to do the dishes. Often it took all the way till noon to get everything done. Then it was already time for the afternoon nap, which my husband got used to during his stay at the hospital in Wiener Neustadt, close to Vienna.

Our relationship became more difficult. I was depressed and angry. Where to find my faith, my devotion, my passion for life, and where to find God's presence within my everyday routine? Is not God my Heavenly Parent? He is the one who gave me this life, being at once Father and Mother. Being a Mom myself, how do I care for my children? It will be with tears, sorrow, deep love, forgiveness, scolding, educating, praying, more tears, and hoping for a happy ending. Our Heavenly Parent must have the same cares for His children with tears, sorrow, deep love, and hoping for a new beginning.

Somehow, I came to realize that the outcome will be what I make of it myself on a daily basis. I have to do my best. But sometimes my best is not good enough.

Then, for a few months, we visited our children in the US and then went to our house in Red Hook. According to the advice of the doctors, Dietrich was on strong medication to thin his blood. He developed a chronic weakness, looking quite sick. But we could not pinpoint what was wrong. I tried to get him to visit holistic doctors, but he refused this possible treatment saying, it will go away, it might be the flu or something similar. I was so worried.

After some soul searching, I called my friend Marie France Kirkley to help me take my husband to the hospital. She came right away. Thank you, Heavenly Father, that Marie France cared so much for our family. With the help of our neighbors, the Wilsons, we transported Dietrich to the car. He almost fainted a few times before he sat down in the vehicle to be driven to Northern Dutchess Hospital in Rhinebeck. I thought to myself, soon he will be in the doctor's care and receive the right treatment.

However, after two gastroscopies to stop the bleeding in his stomach he was not getting better. He continued losing blood and the doctors decided to do an emergency surgery in order to know the cause of his bleeding in the stomach area, and to sew it up. When Dr. Wing came into Dietrich's room to tell him about the surgery, we knew that there was a risk of his passing to the other side because he was so weak and had lost so much blood already.

At this crucial time, I had a surge of energy that we all knew that Dietrich had to fight for his life. He was still in his late sixties, and for me he was simply too young to pass on. So I asked Dr. Wing if it would be all right if I said a prayer before the surgery. The three of us, Dr. Wing, Dietrich and myself, ended up holding hands in prayer, asking God for a successful surgery. Dr. Wing not only had a good reputation professionally, he was also a good man, who had good faith and was simply a man of God.

I asked the angels and former physicians in the spiritual world to help the doctors who were working on my husband to find right away where the bleeding came from, and to repair it instantly. My prayer was directed at Dietrich's survival, that he may have enough strength to go successfully through all the dangers the surgery brought with it. He needed to live longer, because we still had so much to do here on this earth.

The atmosphere was high. We could sense the presence of spiritual beings from a higher realm. Through our hands energy and electricity was passing, as I prayed to Almighty God. Our Heavenly Father was there with us, comforting us by His presence. I also asked for Jesus' help. Sincere, heartfelt prayers with good men and women can be very powerful. It can indeed change the outcome of things.

I was grateful for my daughter and her friend who stayed with me during Dietrich's surgery. Also, Traudl and Marie France were there supporting us. The presence and care of friends, family and other loved ones in difficult times are most precious. We truly needed their presence and loving support. I am eternally grateful for their encouragement and comfort.

After the long surgery, Dr. Wing came to us and said that Dietrich responded well during the operation. He said they fixed the hole in his stomach where he was bleeding. The doctors said that we had to stop those heavy medications.

We went to the intensive care unit to greet Dietrich after his ordeal in the operating room. My husband said that he had three significant dreams that gave him lots of courage for this life on earth.

The first dream was about this physical life, how much we live in fear of each other and that we treat each other based on self-centeredness. Dietrich told us that this first dream was related to his present operation. He was worried that he could not afford the doctor bills in the hospital. Many bills came in and he simply felt inundated by them, feeling helpless to pay everything. Every bill had a voice attached, which seemed to pull out every ounce of energy from him. The whole system was one of heaviness and exploitation. The message was clear for him. This whole system had to change. Instead of worrying all the time what will be next, there should be more understanding from the people surrounding us. Especially if we are sick and hope to be healthy again, we should not be exploited.

The next dream followed the first one immediately. According to Dietrich, what seemed like an experience of the old system was now replaced by a new way of life, where the only rules were compassion, empathy and complete understanding. He told us that the message was clear again, coming directly from the heart of God. It seemed mediated by His good angels. There was no longer any exploitation. He was told, do not worry about the past, but see the brightness of the present. Everything that happened is now forgiven and there will be no sin or separation from God any more. The whole atmosphere was one of caring in a loving way for each other. All our past feelings of shame, guilt and fear were no longer with us, but there were only feelings of indescribable love.

The third dream was an expansion of the previous experience. My husband said that this time there was a winter landscape with lots of white powder snow and many hills.

Dietrich was riding a sleigh with Elisabeth in front and she was giving directions. We had a good speed going up and down the hills. The remarkable thing was the deep joy we could feel while we were riding the sleigh. There was complete harmony in our internal life and externally being fully one with nature. The colors were more beautiful than in regular life. All together it was an exhilarating experience, showing us that so much more is possible than what we expected from our relationships with each other and with mother nature.

Signs from Above

In the early morning, going for my usual walk after some spiritual reading, and conversing, reporting to my husband Dietrich on the one-way phone calls, if I am attentive there is always a greeting, a sign coming from a tree, or the radio, or a word in my heart mind.

Today, my eye caught sight of a beautiful red bird in a bush. A feeling of love and beauty swelled in my heart, a most special greeting, a lovely hello, a sight from beyond the veil.

I came back home and there was a magazine open at a picture of a bright red bird, a cardinal, with the words "Messenger from Heaven."

The page also had the words, "A gentle reminder that we're never far apart, my spirit will live on forever there within your heart." And in my mind, I remembered the words of the song, "And when the time comes, I will be there to meet you and welcome you home."

This reminded me of the time Dietrich found a penny on our morning walk. I told him to keep it; and put it in full view on the small table in our house. The penny reminds me of God and the emblem of America.

Some days the dark is stronger than the light. Still we keep going, keep moving. After a tearful morning prayer, I went for a walk. Suddenly a white truck appeared. On its side was the name of the company, and underneath were the words, "In God We Trust." Definitely God was talking to me: "Trust Me," I will protect you.

Dietrich, Eternal Loving Spouse

The concluding topic of this section, and Elisabeth's whole memoir, is Dietrich, her eternal loving spouse. Her search for true love, the river of her life, led her to this wonderful man in whose eyes she saw God. And here, as Elisabeth writes about, and to, her beloved, she writes about heaven.

The first entries are letters of reflection and resolution that Dietrich and Elisabeth wrote to each other at the conclusion of the year 1997, in preparation for the New Year of 1998. Here we see the great difference in their characters and approaches to life, and also their deep love for, and commitment to, each other.

The next entry, "Our Treasures in Heaven," also shows the differences between them. But love transcends all. Elisabeth recognized what was important to her husband, and accepted that some of the things that she would have enjoyed he would never give her. That was not his way. But his way was more precious than a cup of coffee or even the most beautiful jewels. His way was the way of love for God, for family, and for all humankind. Elisabeth shares her appreciation for this special man eloquently.

Then we reach the entries in which Dietrich's body is failing. Despite the heroic efforts of a special young man who offered his bone marrow, Dietrich's time on earth came to an end. Naturally, for Elisabeth this was heartbreaking.

To ease her pain, she wrote poems, such as "Let's Go Somewhere" and "When the Night Comes." She visited a medium, who shared a beautiful encouraging message: "When you need me, I am around." She writes of her own encounters with Dietrich, in dreams, in words, and feeling his presence. The final entry is a letter she wrote for him recently, concluding that she will love him forever and more. Her search for true love was surely successful.

Concluding 1997

December 31, 1997

Dear Elisabeth,

These last hours of the year 1997 I am dedicating to our Heavenly Father and to you, my precious wife. Maybe one of the deepest insights I had in my relationship to God was the realization that God continues to love us with all His might no matter how much we may feel separated from Him because of our fallen nature. Of course, I may not experience His love because of my fallen past or all the weaknesses and shortcomings I am still struggling with. But the certainty of His love for us is firmly established in my heart and this certainty becomes the source for a still unknown power and strength in the battle against principalities and all kinds of fallen spirits. God's love for us and the reality of all the desires of our original nature then becomes the fertile soil through which we are empowered to bring good fruit for God's kingdom.

This coming year of 1998, I will make a conscious effort to love you as God loves you, to listen to you as God will speak through you, to experience joy through you as God wants to share the joy of His heart with us. Let the year 1998 be the year of accomplishing true love in our marriage Blessing and, in this way, bring abundant fruit for building God's kingdom.

ITN, with all my love

Your husband,

Dietrich

December 31, 1997

To Dietrich

21 years cared for. Appreciate each other. Grateful for good memories.

I like when you are there when I need to talk. I appreciate you listening to me.

I like when you are happy no matter what and cheering everybody up.

I like when you always try to make up after our fights. You do not keep grudges.

I like when you try to take me for walks and time of sharing despite your busy schedule and you would rather work non-stop.

I am grateful for your faith and love for God no matter the persecutions.

I am grateful when you take my opinions into consideration.

I am grateful when you always reassure me that I am the one and only eternal wife.

I am very grateful when you do the dishes, wash the floors.

I am grateful when you take me to restaurants and places.

From Elisabeth

Our Treasures in Heaven

During our married life I often asked my husband "what would you like to eat tonight," and his answer was always the same: "Leftovers."

Not very creative, but somehow he was always very hungry. I learned quickly that I must always have a huge quantity of food. It was not necessary for him for the meal to be delicious or exotic; as long as it was a very big portion, he was satisfied.

He talked often about how his mom would make sugar noodles after the war, when food was still scarce in Vienna.

During World War II, when he was still an infant and the sirens were signaling the population that bomber planes were approaching and every one had to take refuge, his family would run and hide in a basement hoping they would survive. Oma, his mother, told me that Dietrich had pneumonia, but still they had to stay there for long periods of time and shiver with cold. She was afraid her child would not survive.

Finally, they could catch the last boat leaving Vienna on the Danube, and escape to the countryside where Oma could work in a farm and there was more to eat. Life is often dramatic like a novel till the last minute when God intervenes.

Dietrich's grandmother, Leopoldine, had to stay behind. She could hardly feed herself. For a long time, she had only sugar in the home, so she took half a teaspoon in the morning and half a teaspoon in the evening. When they came back after the war her family hardly recognized her. She was so skinny and looking sick, she had to stay in bed most of the time to save her energy.

So perhaps this is one reason why my husband was always so hungry.

One time one of my friends asked me with an accusing tone, why was I feeding my husband leftovers? The point was he never wanted to throw away anything.

In that sense he was always very thrifty. What did he want for his birthday? Nothing at all. Even though we always surprised him with something, he said he does not need anything. I was pleased my daughter and I made sure we had decent and clean clothing for him. His motto was, "One way to save money is not to spend it."

He was generous with others. During our very short engagement, he gave me all the money he had in his pocket. I was so moved by this gesture. I remember wanting to go to a coffee shop one day as we were taking a walk, but he never offered it to me. I wondered why. That was his style.

As for me, I always had a special love for rings, for exotic and beautiful things, that I could never have. My favorite would have been an emerald with the deep green similar to the one I saw in a Vienna museum of jewelry belonging to kings and queens.

But his generosity of heart and care were the deepest; something credit cards can never buy.

He could have been a priest with all the restrictions and vows of poverty. Instead, he chose to have a family, and there kept his eternal vows of fidelity, faithfulness and loving his neighbors more than himself.

This has been more valuable than anything. This is our treasure for all eternity.

Dear Donor

Dear Donor,

Today I am writing to you as the most special person I have ever known.

Only I can write with tears in my eyes for your act of utmost goodness: the gift of life. Words cannot express my gratitude and love for you.

You are so young! You are my new son, truly.

In a way I rejoice to have one more son. I do not know your name but it must be similar to the French name Dieudonné, meaning "Gift of God."

My husband Dietrich, of German-Austrian descent, will receive the bone marrow transplant on May 31, 2016.

I am French, and our marriage was to heal the wounds of war between France and Germany.

I hope you keep well and strong and healthy.

I pray that good fortune and abundant blessings will follow you for the rest of your life!

And know that you are very much loved.

From your new family.

It Is Very Natural

When my husband was in and out of the hospital for chemotherapy and infection, or whatever else, one day out of the blue I asked him bluntly, "Are you scared of dying?" He answered in a very calm voice, "No, it is very natural."

All his life, everything for him has been very natural. If I was in the bathroom saying, "Do not come in, it smells in here," he would reply, "Nein, it is very natural." Or if I couldn't change diapers because my stomach didn't feel right, he would laugh and do it himself. I would always call on him if I saw some creepy spiders and he would remove them. Or a snake in front of our house, he would kill it with a stick.

So, how could I imagine that death was also something natural for him? I could not even entertain till tonight "What am I going to do without him?" I cannot imagine him going away now, not so soon.

But somehow his answer satisfied me. Passing into the next world should be something very natural.

Yes, this is a process like our birth. We first live in the realm of water in the womb. We have to go through the tunnel of the uterus and then the body breathes air. The next world we will breathe love. Many near-death experiences were reported where they go through a tunnel and felt drawn toward the light at the end of the tunnel like a force or an energy calling them. The same for the baby when it is time to come out, the contractions start for the mother and the baby is expelled toward the world of air.

The process of dying for my husband lasted about a year. I was the one feeling always in a crisis. Maybe he is going soon, what shall I do? Today he looked like he is ready to go, what shall I do?

I could witness the chemotherapy was killing him and his immune system. He had no strength whatsoever. It was a vicious circle. Even we tried all-natural therapies; but it was not working. Then he was always on antibiotics because infections came one after the other. He had pneumonia a few times, and the last one he had to have a respirator. I thought this will be just for the night. But it lasted two weeks. I felt the doctors were out of touch with the human being here.

When I am weak, I am strong.

Before you passed, I said: Do not worry. I will take care of everything. Things I do not know about. Things I never did before. Things I do not want to do. Things I am afraid of. Things beyond myself.

But I said: Do not worry. I will take care of everything. How to pay the bills and repair the house. How to write emails and figure out the computer. How to keep in touch and spread love around. How to figure things out without you around. Things left unfinished.

Do not worry I will take care of everything. All the wrongs I will make it right. All the pains I will heal. All the miseries I will make them joys.

Because you left me with a reservoir of true love.

Dietrich and Elisabeth enjoying the beach and the Pacific Ocean

San Diego Beach Where Heaven and Earth Meet

The mystical royal blue Pacific Ocean.

Where the sunny clear sky enters your heart with immense beauty.

You think of eternity. A life without end.

A little more than two years ago Dietrich and I walked on this very beach: La Jolla.

On her way to school where she teaches at the French American school our daughter, Diesa, would drop us off there by the shady park by the beach. She would place a hammock there between two trees for Dietrich to rest.

She did it with filial piety and love, comforting our heart.

Somehow Dietrich still could manage a short walk on the beach holding my arm. He truly enjoyed the natural beauty. We had a lot of "heart therapy" talks.

Deep down without admitting it, I knew he was going to go.

And I was going to stay.

This is the place I think I asked him, are you scared to die?

He said he was not. This is something very natural.

I walked there again yesterday. Beautiful beach, same ocean.

Dietrich still holding my arm from above.

This is the place in America where Heaven and Earth meet.

This is the place where we offered many prayers.

The place where prayers are answered now.

Or in hundred years.

But they are answered.

Let's Go Somewhere

> Where the sky is more blue
> Where the sun is shining bright
> Somewhere where you can love me more
> Somewhere nice.
> Somewhere far,
> Or close by.
> Where the moon is full
> And the stars fill the night.
> Take me somewhere else.
> Where God lives.
> Where I can see His face, and tears of joy.
> The place where He meets his children.
> You'll be there.
> And I will come with you.
> Take me there.

When I Need You, You Are Around

> From an evening at the Enchanted Café in Red Hook, NY, April 18, 2018

A message for Elisabeth from Dietrich, received by a local psychic medium.

You said, you do not want to make me cry.

Already there is a tear drop in my eye.

You said: When you need me, I will be around.

You said, you are sorry you left too soon. You left things you did not want to, like the bills to pay. You did not want to leave at this difficult moment. Even you could not imagine being somewhere without me, without holding my hand.

You said, I am your girl for all eternity and when I need you, you'll be around.

You said, the best thing about our fights was when we were making peace.

You call me sweet names, and I am your girl for all eternity.

Over there, there is no time, there is no space.

When I go there, you said you'll be there to welcome me. You'll be there for me. For you it is tomorrow, for me many more years.

You said, I can feel you. I call you sweet names. I am so grateful you are taking care of things and everybody, and our extended family.

I am your girl for all eternity.

You passed. But you said you could hear everything. You were there at your funeral. You were there when I made a meal for you.

You call me sweet names. I am your girl for all eternity. You said when you need me, I am around.

I Had a Dream

When the going gets tough, the tough get going, as they say. I try to keep going since my husband passed. But some days are really tough.

So, I have been talking to Dietrich on the other side. I told him, "I did not see you for soooo very long, where are you? Why don't you come in my dreams?"

So, he did. In a vivid color dream, he appeared shortly with a huge happy smile.

We touched hands, but it was another substance. Same touch same feeling, but another substance. It is hard to describe, like rubber and transparent. But I did touch his hands and it was a beautiful encounter.

The Stadt Park in Vienna

May 4, 2018

I arrived in Vienna, Austria, last week, with the American delegation for the "Peace Starts with Me" festival. Always with emotion I remember the city of my late husband. I heard him in my spirit heart saying, "I hope you feel a little bit at home in Vienna." I heard him because it was the tone and the words he would say to me.

After a few days there in the Austrian capital, our nephew Sami informed me that Dietrich's mom, Oma, 97 years young was brought to the hospital because of another fall. She also became a bit confused. I was asked to wait till they called me again to see the best time to visit. After two days I became a little impatient and tried to call the nephews and nieces, but no answer.

I was in the Stadt park, just minutes away from St Elizabeth/Franziskus Hospital, I was pondering what to do. Perhaps I should just go in front of Oma's door and pray there without disturbing her.

Then I heard again Dietrich's voice in my spirit heart: "Let's go now, together."

So we went. As I approached Oma's room, a nurse was going in, so Dietrich said, "Let's go in together." So I (we) went in.

Dietrich's sister Gisela was there also and recognized me it seemed (she has beginning stages of Alzheimer's) and was so happy to see me. The three of us hugged, including Margaretha Vesely, Oma, Dietrich's Mom.

Then Oma asked me who I was, even though she has known me since our marriage. Then Gisela repeated the question, who am I? I responded simply, I am Dietrich's wife.

Then Oma took my both hands and asked, "Are you really Dietrich's wife?" Yes, Oma, I am. Then she became very excited and happy. "She is Dietrich's wife, oh my God, oh my God!" She took my hands again.

It was a happy family reunion, where we could sense the angels and people we love from the spirit world enjoying the love we shared.

The Stadt Park is close to Dietrich's home and had been his playground when he was a child, and the place he would take a break from his studies as a teenager. No wonder it was there that he met a missionary from the Unification Church. It was 50 years ago this September 1st, close to Johann Strauss' statue, by the pond where the clock is.

It is there too, when we lived in Vienna, that we ended up our days, after visiting his family and after his classes at the International University or Webster University. We had many walks there. The trees remember us, and also the pond and the statues and the grass. We deeply enjoyed this place. Everything in nature remembers every single word we utter in prayer. As for us, walks mean prayers. Prayers mean walks.

In this place full of Dietrich's presence, I could hear my beloved's voice.

When the Night Comes

For Dietrich, Christmas 2018

> When it's cold outside
> Please embrace me
>   and hug me.
> Do not let go of my hand,
> hold me tight.
> Do not go anywhere
> Just stay here with me
>   When the night comes.
> Baby, it's cold outside
> Do not let go of me
> Hold me more tight
> Let your love warm me up.
> Let's make popcorn
> And talk together
> till morning comes.
> Hug me again.
> Embrace me.
> Just stay here with me
> till the sun rises
> And all the lonely night is gone.

Love Needs to be Expressed Over and Over and Beyond this World

One night I woke up in the early morning, around 2 or 4, with this sentence ringing in my head, repeating itself very loudly and directed towards me:

"I will give all my love for you, always."

"I will give all my love for you, always."

It is very reassuring to know your true love never ever dies, and he is there with you, visiting you, checking on you, and loving you for ever and ever and more.

I love you.

I love you too.

I love you more.

Love can never be felt alone.

Dear Dietrich

Dear Dietrich, when I opened my wallet this morning to search for my I.D. card for some paper work at the office for the pension, I saw your picture first. Every time I see your picture, I feel a pinch in my heart.

I love you the same as 41 years ago when I first met you.

Then I opened my notebook to look for an address, and the words written on the first page jumped up to my eyes. These are your last words to me before you went: "I will be always with you, forever together." I felt another pinch in my heart as those words came to me like a waterfall over and over again.

The next thing I felt you were right there with me, drinking some coffee. And if I feel your presence next to me like in the past, I cannot hold my tears dropping in my coffee.

How can one live without love? Even if you are gone to the other side, you can still visit me. And even though I do not see you, I sense you are here. Because when you are here the vibrations, the spiritual atmosphere is very high, and I learned to recognize it.

You are here, always hopeful, always joyful, always giving, always loving.

How can one be without love? Without sharing the deepest part of oneself to the other, or even have no one to rely on?

Dietrich and Elisabeth, true love couple forever

I sense God, my Heavenly Parent, whom I love and I want everyone to love and be loved by.

This is the reason I want to share the Blessing that I received with everyone I meet. That only tears of joy will melt hearts together because from now on God will be in every Blessed relationship. And the evil and misuse of love which has plagued humanity with distress and sorrow will be gone forever, because God can finally reach everyone. Why?

Because the True Parents, the Only Begotten Son and the Only Begotten Daughter of God, have been here showing the way of true love. And the beast from the book of Revelation has finally been strangled.

This is why the love of God can reach everyone now.

Dietrich, I love you forever and more.

Your eternal wife, Elisabeth

"Mom is patient, mom is kind. She does not envy, she does not boast, she is not proud. She is not rude, she is not self-seeking, she is not easily angered, she keeps no record of wrongs. Mom does not delight in evil but rejoices with the truth. She always protects, always trusts, always hopes, always perseveres.
   Mom never fails."
                    1 Elisabeth 13:4-8

Recommended Readings

Byrne, Lorna. *A Message of Hope from the Angels*. Atria Books, 2012.

Garlow, James L., and Keith Wall. *Heaven and the Afterlife*. Bethany House Publishers, 2009.

Mark, Barbara, and Trudy Griswold. *Angelspeake: How to Talk with Your Angels*. Simon & Schuster, 1995.

Mickler, Michael L. *Forty Years in America: An Intimate History of the Unification Movement, 1959-1999*. HSA Publications, 2000.

Moon, Sun Myung. *Exposition of the Divine Principle*. HSA Publications, 1996.

Moon, Sun Myung. *As a Peace-Loving Global Citizen*. The Washington Times Foundation, 2010.

Seidel, Dietrich F., and Elisabeth M. Seidel. Edited by Jennifer P. Tanabe. *Beloveds Forever Together: Letters of Eternal Love.* Lulu, 2017.

Seidel, Dietrich F., and Jennifer P. Tanabe. *Eternal Life in the Spirit World*. Lulu, 2017.

Sherwood, Carlton. *Inquisition: The Persecution and Prosecution of the Reverend Sun Myung Moon*. Regnery Publishing, 1991.

Spurgin, Nora M. *Circles of Angels: How You Can Call Your Own Circle of Angels to Energize Your Life*. HSA Publications, 2017.

Tanabe, Jennifer P. (ed.). *The Ideal Family to Be or Not to Be: Testimonies of a Life of Faith, A Biography of David S.C. Kim*. Lulu, 2010.

Tanabe, Jennifer P. (ed.). *Unification Insights into Marriage and Family: The Writings of Dietrich F. Seidel*. Lulu, 2016.

Tanabe, Jennifer P. (ed.) *Spiritual Guidance for Daily Life: Sermons by Dietrich F. Seidel*. Lulu, 2018.

Wilson, Andrew (ed.). *The Fruits of True Love: The Life Work of Reverend Sun Myung Moon*. Paragon House, 2000.